Applying a Pers
Approach to El
Criteri

Applying a Personalised Approach to Eligibility Criteria

Daisy Bogg

Open University Press

Open University Press
McGraw-Hill Education
McGraw-Hill House
Shoppenhangers Road
Maidenhead
Berkshire
England
SL6 2QL

email: enquiries@openup.co.uk
world wide web: www.openup.co.uk

and Two Penn Plaza, New York, NY 10121–2289, USA

First published 2012

A catalogue record of this book is available from the British Library

ISBN-13: 978-0-33-524515-4 (pb)
ISBN-10: 0-33-524515-3 (pb)
eISBN: 978-0-33-524516-1

Library of Congress Cataloging-in-Publication Data
CIP data applied for

Typesetting and e-book compilations by
RefineCatch Limited, Bungay, Suffolk
Printed in Great Britain by CPI Group (UK) Ltd, Croydon, CRO 4YY

The *McGraw·Hill* Companies

Contents

How to use this book

This pocketbook is designed to help guide you through the process of applying social care eligibility criteria to psychosocial needs within the context of personalisation. The book can be dipped in and out of as needed, and provides a range of complementary yet stand-alone aspects, from setting out the legal and policy framework and its application to social work practice, through to exploring different domains and how these can be assessed and evidenced.

Chapter 1 provides a summary of the various frameworks that social care operates and how these are applied to individual and personalised social care provision.

Chapter 2 considers the Fair Access to Care Services (FACS) criteria and explores how the various domains apply to assess psychosocial needs and develop social care support.

Chapter 3 considers the psychosocial domains of NHS Continuing Healthcare and how the health and social care eligibility frameworks may interact and overlap.

Chapter 4 of this pocketbook moves on to providing general help and guidance to support good practice, including highlighting some of the main pitfalls experienced by practitioners and provides a range of examples to illustrate how eligibility criteria can be applied to support a personalised approach to psychosocial needs.

The final chapter provides details of some of the resources you can use to help maintain and develop your practice. These consider both your overall knowledge base and your specific skills. They are intended to give you some initial signposts from which further reading and resources can be accessed.

1 Social care in context

The aim of this pocketbook is to support social work practitioners is assessing and applying eligibility criteria for social care support where individual needs are of a complex or psychosocial nature. When undertaking social work tasks in relation to service user and carer eligibility it can be helpful to understand the context and frameworks in which you are working, and as such this first chapter provides an overview of the policy framework and explores key terms and themes that shape the social care agenda in England. Many texts have been written about the development of community care (see Mandelstam 2009; Clements and Thompson 2011), and this pocketbook is not seeking to replicate these accounts but rather provide an overview of what is currently in place.

Community care can be a complex area to navigate, particularly when the individual's needs are multiple and/or psychosocial in nature. Within the current system, local authorities (LA), or Local Social Services Authorities (LSSA), have both duties and powers to consider and exercise. In the context of social care service provision, these terms are clearly set out and defined as:

■ *duty*: The authority must act as set out in the legal framework.
■ *power*: The authority can act but it is not compelled to do so.

Law and policy, which consists of primary and secondary legislation (i.e. Acts of Parliament and Rules and Regulations) together with government guidance, which must be followed by local authorities save in exceptional circumstances, provide the framework for the provision of social services. Each Local Authority is required to interpret this framework and apply systems, policies and procedures to meet the needs of their local population, ensuring that these reflect the national legal and policy position.

There are two key areas that social workers need to be aware of within the context of adult social care, first, the assessment of a person's needs, and, second, in light of the outcome of that assessment, the decision to provide (or not) services to meet those needs. Both of these activities are carried out within a legal framework, and social workers will need to be aware of this when undertaking their roles.

THE LEGAL CONTEXT OF ASSESSMENT

Social care services in England are the responsibility of Local Social Services Authorities (LSSAs), of which there are 152 across the country. Each LSSA has a defined geographical boundary within which it is responsible for a whole range of local community needs, including assessing and providing services to individuals and families, who, for whatever reason, may be in need of support.

Before an LSSA can decide whether someone is eligible for social care support, they need to identify the individual's needs, and for this an assessment is required. This assessment is carried out under the legal framework provided by the NHS and Community Care Act 1990, which states under Section 47:

> where it appears to a local authority that any person for whom they may provide or arrange for the provision of community care services may be in need of any such services, the authority –
> (a) shall carry out an assessment of his needs for those services; and
> (b) having regard to the results of that assessment, shall then decide whether his needs call for the provision by them of any such services.

Under this section, the LSSA has to decide whether the individual may be in need of community care services. Most authorities operate some kind of screening process to determine whether an individual meets this threshold and to determine the type and urgency of the assessment that needs to be carried out.

While the NHS and Community Care Act 1990 is the significant piece of legislation in terms of setting out the duties of LSSAs to assess individuals who may be in need of services, duties under several other pieces of legislation are also in place, these are:

- *The NHS and Community Care Act 1990, Section 47(2).* If the person is identified as being 'disabled', that person has additional rights that require the LSSA to make a decision as to the services required under Section 4 of the Disabled Persons (Services and Consultation and Representation) Act 1986.
- *Disabled Persons (Services and Consultation and Representation) Act 1986, Section 4.* This imposes a duty on local authorities to decide whether the needs of a disabled person call for the provision by the Local Authority of any services in accordance with Section 2(1) of the Chronically Sick and Disabled Persons Act 1970.
- *Chronically Sick and Disabled Persons Act 1970, Section 2.* This places a duty on local authorities to assess the individual needs of everyone who falls within Section 29 of the National Assistance Act 1948 (see Point of Law box on p. 6 for details of the types of services included).
- *National Assistance Act 1948, Section 29(1).* To qualify for services under this section, persons must be: 'aged 18 or over who are blind, deaf, or dumb, or who suffer from mental disorder of any description, and other persons aged 18 or over who are substantially and permanently handicapped by illness, injury, congenital deformity or such other disabilities as may be prescribed by the Minister'.
- *The Carers and Disabled Children Act 2000, Section 6.* This section provides that a person with parental responsibility for a disabled child has the right to an assessment from the Local

Authority of their ability to provide (and to continue to provide) care for the child. The Local Authority must take that assessment into account when deciding what services, if any, to provide under Section 17 of the Children Act 1989.

■ *Disabled Persons (Services Consultation and Representation) Act 1986, Section 8*. Carers also have rights under this section which requires local councils to have regard to the ability of the carer to provide or continue to provide care when deciding which services to provide to the disabled person. In these circumstances, the assessment of the cared-for person must take account of the carers situation and record this as part of the assessment of the cared-for person. This requirement exists even where the caring role is not of a regular or substantial nature.

Good Practice Point: Know the Legislation

Make sure you know what legislation you are acting under before you undertake your assessment. Being clear of the remit of your role is an important aspect of professional practice and ensures the information you give to service users and carers about their rights to assessment is accurate and based on the legal framework.

THE LEGAL CONTEXT OF DELIVERING SERVICES

Once an assessment has been carried out, the LSSA will need to decide which, if any, services will be provided to meet the assessed needs. Provision of services takes place primarily under the following pieces of legislation:

- *National Assistance Act 1948, Section 21(1)*. Concerns the provision of residential accommodation to certain groups of people over 18 years who through age, illness, disability or any other circumstances are in need of care and attention which would otherwise be unavailable to them. The duty is owed to people 'ordinarily resident' in the Local Authority's area.
- *National Assistance Act 1948, Section 29*. The local council has a *duty* to exercise its powers for people 'ordinarily resident' in its area and must provide:
    - a social work advice and support service;
    - facilities for rehabilitation and adjustment to disability;
    - facilities for occupational, social, cultural and recreational activities.
- *Chronically Sick and Disabled Person's Act 1970, Section 1*. This section imposes a *duty* on local authorities to provide information about relevant services.
- *Chronically Sick and Disabled Person's Act 1970, Section 2(1)*. This section sets out the types and range of services that local councils should have available to meet the needs of 'disabled people' (see Point of Law box).
- *National Health Services Act 1977, Section 21*. This section identifies that services can be provided in relation to expectant mothers, prevention and after care, and that home help and laundry facilities are functions exercisable by social service authorities. Schedule 8 identifies the *power* to provide and maintain day centres or similar facilities and *power* to arrange services specifically for people with alcohol and drug problems. Also to provide laundry services as part of the input of home help services.
- *Mental Health Act 1983, Section 117(2)*. This section creates a joint *duty* on the local Health and Social Services Authorities to provide after-care services to various categories of people who have been detained in hospital for treatment for mental disorder (Sections 3, 7, 17a) for as long as the person needs them. After-care

services are not defined in the Act but include social work support in helping the ex-patient with problems of accommodation or family relationships, the provision of domiciliary services and the use of day centre and residential facilities.

■ *Community Care (Direct Payments) 1996 Act.* This sets out the circumstances when Direct Payments should be considered. It gives local authorities the *power* to offer people cash payments as an alternative to arranging social care services to meet their assessed, eligible needs.

■ *Health Services Act 1968, Section 45.* The Local Authority has the *power* to make arrangements to promote the welfare of older people.

■ *The Carers and Disabled Children Act 2000, Section 2.* Under this section the Local Authority has *powers* to provide services for carers following a carer's assessment (whether joint or separate) under Section 1 of this Act. Services to carers are not defined by the Act. The Local Authority has the *power* to provide any services as they see fit and which in their view help the carer care for the person cared for.

■ *The Carers and Disabled Children Act 2000, Section 5.* This section extends the option of Direct Payments to carers aged 16 years or over who care for a person aged 18 or over.

Point of Law: Chronically Sick and Disabled Persons Act 1970

Section 2: Provision of welfare services

1   Where a local authority having functions under section 29 of the National Assistance Act 1948 are satisfied in the case of any person to whom that section applies who is ordinarily resident in their area that it is necessary in order to meet the needs of that person for that authority to make arrangements for all or any of the following matters, namely –

(a) the provision of practical assistance for that person in his home;

(b) the provision for that person of, or assistance to that person in obtaining, wireless, television, library or similar recreational facilities;

(c) the provision for that person of lectures, games, outings or other recreational facilities outside his home or assistance to that person in taking advantage of educational facilities available to him;

(d) the provision for that person of facilities for, or assistance in, travelling to and from his home for the purpose of participating in any services provided under arrangements made by the authority under the said section 29 or, with the approval of the authority, in any services provided otherwise than as aforesaid which are similar to services which could be provided under such arrangements;

(e) the provision of assistance for that person in arranging for the carrying out of any works of adaptation in his home or the provision of any additional facilities designed to secure his greater safety, comfort or convenience;

(f) facilitating the taking of holidays by that person, whether at holiday homes or otherwise and whether provided under arrangements made by the authority or otherwise;

(g) the provision of meals for that person whether in his home or elsewhere;

(h) the provision for that person of, or assistance to that person in obtaining, a telephone and any special equipment necessary to enable him to use a telephone.

Good Practice Point: Know Your Own Remit

Make sure you know which legislation you are acting under before you make any recommendations or decisions about what services would best meet the individual's needs. Being clear of the remit of your role is an important aspect of professional practice and ensures the information you give to service users and carers about their rights to services is accurate and based on their entitlements.

PERSONALISATION AND TRANSFORMING ADULT SOCIAL CARE

Changes in both society and the way services were delivered, higher expectations and an increasing evidence base, which demonstrated that better outcomes could be achieved if individuals were enabled to take greater ownership of their own situations, ultimately led to the publication of the White Paper, *Our Health, Our Care, Our Say* (DOH 2006), the first significant joint health and social care policy published by the UK central government. This White Paper, was published following extensive consultation and its vision of social care was based upon that set out in the previous Green Paper, *Independence, Well-Being and Choice* (DOH 2005). Both the Green and White Papers were underpinned by the principle that every individual had 'a positive contribution to make to society and a right to control their own lives' (DOH 2006: 9) and, as such, service provision needed to be refocused.

In 2008, the cross-governmental concordat *Putting People First* (HM Government 2007) was published, followed by a Local Authority Circular (DOH 2008) which set out the continued commitment to the vision of adult social care and clarified the expectations of local authorities in terms of reforming the community care system for adults. *Putting People First* marked the start of the most significant reform in social care since the introduction of community care in the 1990s, and continues to pose a challenge to both social workers and their employing organisations in terms of making it a reality in local areas. Four areas of focus are identified within the personalised approach (HM Government 2007), these are:

1   *Universal Services*: Services that are accessible to all should be developed and supported to provide services for those with additional social care needs.
2   *Early Intervention and Prevention*: Low threshold services designed to minimise the risk to the community and/or individual independence.

3   *Choice and Control*: Service users and carers are able to shape and lead their support to maximise independence.
4   *Social Capital*: Community resources and informal support networks are developed and supported, with individuals supported to participate within their own community.

Example from Practice

Sadie was diagnosed with bipolar disorder and had periods of being very manic and other times when she was very depressed and unable to take part in daily and community activities. When she was well, Sadie had a volunteer job at her local community centre where she helped with the catering for a twice-weekly lunch club and organised a monthly coffee morning and table-top sale. These roles helped Sadie to have social contact, provided her with routine and the opportunity to use her skills, all aspects which helped her to better manage her mental health. Sadie had been admitted to hospital a number of times in the past when she became manic, as she was considered to be at risk in terms of her health and safety and also was vulnerable to exploitation. She found hospital admission very traumatic and the disruption to her community activities and daily activities was very severe.

Sadie was assessed under the NHS and Community Care Act 1990 and it was identified that she was in need of services as a result of her mental health. The aim was to support her ongoing recovery and minimise the need for intensive and hospital-based services.

Under Fair Access to Care Services (FACS) (see Chapter 2), Sadie was assessed as having eligible needs in relation to her community and family life and daily and personal routines, which in turn impacted upon her needs in the domains of autonomy and choice. As a result she was considered to be in substantial need under FACS and social care support was agreed.

Sadie was allocated a personal budget amount based on her eligible needs and, working with her care coordinator, she identified that access to additional support would be of benefit when she was experiencing

> relapse and that this, combined with alternative therapies (in this instance, acupuncture and yoga instruction), would support her ongoing mental health and potentially prevent a full-blown relapse that might result in a hospital admission.
>
> Sadie and her care coordinator agreed a support plan which included support mechanisms that could be accessed if Sadie felt she needed them, which increased her choice and control, and regular activities which contributed to both her overall well-being and assisted her to sustain her community activities, supporting her to continue to build social capital and based upon a preventative approach.

With the increased recognition that social involvement and community integration are essential elements of individual well-being as well as being a means of meeting needs that cannot be met (or are not appropriate to being met) via social care funding and services. Carer support and preventative services are central themes, with the aim being to support and develop community responses and initiatives rather than attempting to spread stretched public resources.

In reality, both the concordat and subsequent policy documents and toolkits published to support the implementation of personalised social care have acknowledged that many aspects of the approach are difficult to achieve. In addition, the learning from previous attempts at increasing service user control, for example, Direct Payments, which were initially introduced in 1998 and failed to achieve the intended take-up, illustrates that there are many challenges to overcome in making the aspiration into a reality, and the eligibility framework provided by FACS is one of these challenges. On the one hand, local authorities are required to focus on prevention and increasing choice and, on the other, the eligibility thresholds are being increased as councils struggle to manage pressurised budgets.

Following a change in government in 2010, the Conservative/Liberal Democrat Coalition published their vision of adult social care (DOH

2010c) entitled *A Vision for Adult Social Care: Capable Communities and Active Citizens* which set out a continuing commitment to the personalisation agenda, and highlighted the government's commitment to three key areas for attention:

- breaking down barriers between health and social care funding to incentivise preventative action;
- extending the greater roll-out of personal budgets to give people and their carers more control and purchasing power; and
- using Direct Payments to carers and better community-based provision to improve access to respite care.

The focus on personalisation remains a government priority, and local authorities are continuing to develop and deliver personalised services with an emphasis on universal services and social capital within their business and partnership plans. The strategic vision for this agenda varies across local areas, with LAs retaining autonomy in terms of how they apply the requirements to meet the needs of their populations. As a social worker responsible for assessing, brokering and delivering services, it is good practice to ensure you are fully aware of your authority's plans and priorities and the thresholds that are in place. This knowledge will assist you in ensuring that the service users and carers you support are able to access the support, services and finances that they are entitled to.

Good Practice Point: Know Your Authority's Personalisation Plans

Familiarise yourself with your Local Authority's personalisation plans to make sure your practice is up to date and maximises resources for service users.

THE FUTURE OF SOCIAL CARE

In the past decade successive governments have been acutely aware that in the context of an ageing society, combined with the economic impacts of recession and interest rates on savings and pensions, the demands upon the care system are not financially sustainable. A number of proposals, consultations and reviews have been carried out to attempt to identify a preferred option – the most recent of these being by the Dilnot Commission.

The Dilnot Commission presents the most recent of a number of criticisms that have been levelled at the FACS system in terms of its application and implementation in local areas. However, the 2010 guidance retained the framework with a view to alignment with the personalised approach rather than redesigning a system that shares the values and principles of today's social care priorities. It is unclear at this time which reforms will be implemented, however, it may be that the updated 2010 FACS guidance will be reviewed again in response to the Commission's recommendations.

 Point of Policy: The Dilnot Commission on Eligibility Criteria

The current system is also confusing, unfair and unsustainable. Assessment processes are complex and opaque; eligibility varies depending on where you live and there is no portability if you move between local authorities. Provision of information and advice is poor, and services often fail to join up. All this means that people frequently do not have good experiences.
(Dilnot Commission 2011b: 1)

We recommend that eligibility criteria for service entitlement should be set on a standardised national basis to improve

consistency and fairness across England, and that there should be
portability of assessments. In the short term, we think it is
reasonable for a minimum eligibility threshold to be set nationally
at 'substantial' under the current system. The Government should
also urgently develop a more objective eligibility and assessment
framework.

(Dilnot Commission 2011a: 6)

WHAT IS ELIGIBILITY?

The duty to undertake an assessment is a requirement that all LSSAs
are required to respond to under this Act. However, qualifying for services will be determined by the eligibility criteria applied by the Local
Authority – where services are provided, the individual will be considered as having 'eligible needs' and once these have been identified an
authority has a duty to provide services or support to meet these needs.
Finite resources are available to respond to social care needs and, as
such, councils need to be able to manage the available budgets in order
to provide services for their populations and ensure those with the
most severe needs are able to access appropriate funding and
services.

Following a number of court challenges during the late 1990s, the
courts confirmed that LSSAs were able to take into account available
resources when setting eligibility rules, however, that once a person is
assessed as having needs that meet the locally set criteria, an authority
has a duty to meet that need (*R v Gloucestershire County Council, ex
parte Barry* 1997). In 2002, the Department of Health issued a Local
Authority Circular (LAC) to LSSAs on eligibility for social care services, detailing the framework, entitled *Fair Access to Care Services*
(DOH 2002). Practice guidance to support the implementation of the
framework was published in 2003. This guidance was consistent with
court findings, and LSSAs were required to develop local policies,

which could be amended from time to time with local consultation. The guidance was updated in 2010 (DOH 2010a) to reflect the developments within the personalisation agenda and reflect the changes that had occurred in social care since the original guidance was issued.

Fair Access to Care Services (FACS) is effectively a means to prioritise and allocate resources to those assessed as being in the highest need of social care support, by providing a consistent approach that LSSAs could apply which would help to address inequalities and discrepancies in funding arrangements across the country.

The framework is split into four bands – low, moderate, substantial and critical (see Figure 1.1) – which are assessed in terms of the risk to an individual's independence as a result of a range of social care need domains. The Fair Access to Care bandings were originally set out in 2002 (DOH 2002) and the updated guidance (DOH 2010a) reconfirmed this approach. While local authorities are able to determine their own policies in relation to providing services and the use of the resources they have available, these must take account of national guidance.

Guidance on the eligibility of carers to receive social care services was issued in 2001 within the practice guidance for the Carers and Disabled Children Act 2000 (DOH 2001). This guidance sets out a requirement for LSSAs to ensure their eligibility criteria for carers' assessment were clear and published, and stated 'the key factors of sustainability to the caring role and the extent of risk should be the basis of the eligibility framework that local authorities should implement' (DOH 2001: 30).

FACS does not require LSSAs to provide services to everyone regardless of the banding they are assessed within, but rather the aim of the FACS guidance was not to standardise services, but rather to ensure 'that individuals with similar difficulties received similar outcomes' (DOH 2002: 3) by providing the strategic framework that would be applied and thus minimising inequalities that could occur due to different LSSA approaches and resource allocation priorities.

Critical
- Life is, or will be threatened,
- Significant health problems have or will develop,
- Serious abuse or neglect has or will occur,
- Inability to carry out vital personal care or domestic routines,
- Vital involvement in work, education or learning cannot or will not be sustained,
- Vital social support systems and relationships cannot or will not be sustained,
- Vital family and social roles/responsibilities cannot or will not be undertaken.

Substantial
- There is, or will be, only partial control over the immediate environment,
- Abuse or neglect has or will occur,
- There is, or will be, an inability to carry out the majority of personal care or domestic routines,
- Involvement in many aspects of work, education or learning cannot or will not be sustained,
- The majority of social support systems and relationships cannot or will not be sustained,
- The majority of family and social roles/responsibilities cannot or will not be undertaken.

Independence

Moderate
- There is, or will be, an inability to carry out several personal care or domestic routines,
- Involvement in several aspects of work, education or learning cannot or will not be sustained,
- Several social support systems and relationships cannot or will not be sustained,
- Several family and other social roles and responsibilities cannot or will not be undertaken.

Low
- There is, or will be, an inability to carry out one or two personal care or domestic routines,
- Involvement in one or two aspects of work, education or learning cannot or will not be sustained,
- One or two support systems and relationships cannot or will not be sustained,
- One or two family and other social roles/responsibilities cannot or will not be undertaken.

Figure 1.1 Fair Access to Care Services eligibility bandings

Good Practice Point: Know How to Apply FACS

Before undertaking your assessment, make sure you are familiar with your Local Authority's policies and procedures for applying FACS. Which bandings does your Local Authority provide services for, and what are the local thresholds in use?

The domains that are considered by FACS include both physical and psychosocial needs, and take a holistic view of an individual's situation (Figure 1.2). These domains provide the foundation of individual independence, and the assessment process should include how these needs and risks could change over time and the likely outcomes if support is not provided. Consideration of these risks should include not only the individual, but also carers and the wider family, where appropriate.

Good Practice Point: Risk to Independence

Remember that FACS applies to the risk to independence NOT the risk of harm or other incidents. It is important to consider the person's independence and aspirations as the central element of an FACS assessment if you are to appropriately apply the criteria.

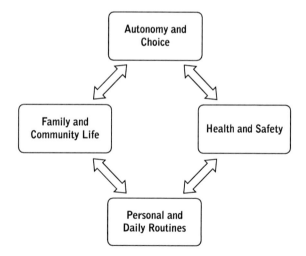

Figure 1.2 The FACS domains

NHS CONTINUING HEALTHCARE

In many cases it is not a straightforward task to separate an individual's health and social care needs, particularly in complex situations such as mental health and other cognitive issues. As with FACS, it is important for practitioners to be aware of the policy framework surrounding healthcare, as it may be that the needs of a service user span both frameworks and it is important to consider what is the most appropriate sources of support in each case.

The NHS and Community Care Act 1990 places a responsibility on local authorities to notify the relevant Primary Care Trust (PCT) if it is identified in assessment that the person has needs which may fall under the National Health Service Act 2006 (see Point of Law box), and invite the PCT to assist in the assessment process (NHS Community Care Act 1990, Section 47(3)(a)) where this is the case.

 Point of Law: National Health Service Act 2006

Section 47(3): Secretary of State's duty as to the provision of certain services

1 The Secretary of State must provide throughout England, to such extent as he considers necessary to meet all reasonable requirements –
   (a) hospital accommodation;
   (b) other accommodation for the purpose of any service provided under this Act;
   (c) medical, dental, ophthalmic, nursing and ambulance services;
   (d) such other services or facilities for the care of pregnant women, women who are breastfeeding, and young children as he considers are appropriate as part of the health service;

(e) such other services or facilities for the prevention of illness, the care of persons suffering from illness, and the after-care of persons who have suffered from illness as he considers are appropriate as part of the health service;

(f) such other services or facilities for the diagnosis and treatment of illness.

Continuing Healthcare is the system of NHS funding for individuals who are assessed as having a primary health need and who require after-care or ongoing healthcare (either accommodated in hospital or within the community). This may be instead of, or as well as, social care support needs, and social workers will be required to consider which set of criteria best matches the individual's needs.

Whether someone has a 'primary health need' is assessed by looking at all the individual's needs and relating them to four key indicators:

- *Nature*: this describes the characteristics and type of the individual's needs and the overall effect these needs have on the individual, including the type of interventions required to manage those needs.
- *Complexity*: this is about how the individual's needs present and interact, and the level of skill required to monitor the symptoms, treat the condition and/or manage the care.
- *Intensity*: this is the extent and severity of the individual's needs and the support needed to meet them, which includes the need for sustained/ongoing care.
- *Unpredictability*: this is about how hard it is to predict changes in an individual's needs that might create challenges in managing them, including the risks to the individual's health if adequate and timely care is not provided (NHS 2009).

Chapter 3 of this pocketbook will look at the criteria for NHS Continuing Healthcare in more detail.

Good Practice Point: Continuing Healthcare Contact

Do you know who your Continuing Healthcare contact point is at your local PCT? Would you know who to contact if you identified a healthcare need within your assessment?

SUMMARY

This chapter aimed to provide an overview of the policy and legal frameworks that social care operates within so that readers have an understanding of the complexities of the current system. Eligible needs are sometimes a difficult concept to capture, especially where Local Authority thresholds differ, and thus the remainder of this book is designed to support practitioners in their assessments, and provide guidance concerning how complex and multiple needs can be applied to the FACS criteria. Local policies and procedures will influence how social workers deal with eligibility; however, there are a range of common themes that should be considered which will be explored in Chapter 2.

Reminder Checklist: Social Care Policy

✓ Are you clear about which legal and policy framework you are following to undertake assessments or provide services?

✓ Are you clear about which rights and entitlements the service user and carer have within your assessment process?

✓ Have you familiarised yourself with your Local Authority's policies and procedures on eligibility?

✓ Have you familiarised yourself with your local authority's policies and procedures on personalisation?

✓ Have you reviewed your own assessment practice to make sure you are taking into account the various frameworks in place?

2 Fair Access to Care Services (FACS)

Personalisation as a method of delivery of social care has posed a number of challenges to both local authorities and social work practitioners. It can appear that the focus on person-centred approaches and individual choice and control is at times in opposition to tightening eligibility thresholds and dwindling resources. Social workers can find themselves at a loss in terms of how to balance conflicting priorities, and this chapter will explore these issues and consider how personalised support planning can be matched to the current FACS criteria.

Expenditure in England on social care illustrates that older people remain the highest proportion of service users in receipt of social care funding support. The NHS Information Centre publishes annual data on expenditure and unit costs and the 2009/10 information is provided in Figure 2.1.

Older people, people with a learning disability and physical disability are the groups that receive the highest level of support from social services. It could be suggested that it is more straightforward to assess eligibility for these groups as there is often a clear impairment which impacts on either the individual's health and safety or their ability to undertake personal care. These criteria are clear in that someone either can or cannot undertake certain tasks. Where the need is not quite as black or white, or where a need is fluctuating, it can be more difficult to make a case for support under the funding criteria.

The four domains of FACS each need to be considered in terms of the individual's physical, psychological and social needs. In order to be assessed as eligible, the social worker needs to be satisfied that the individual's presenting needs meet the Local Authority's threshold for support. A personalised support plan can complicate

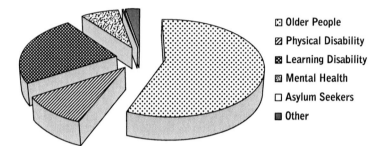

Figure 2.1 Social care expenditure by service user group (2009/10)

Source: Adapted from NHS Information Centre (2011).

these considerations as social workers are increasingly asked to consider social inclusion, the individual's wishes and aspirations, the wider family and the community, and preventative options, many of which do not meet the higher banding of eligibility.

In terms of process, once an assessment has been made which indicates that the individual's needs are considered eligible under FACS, agreement for funding support is required. In some areas this may be via a local manager and in others it will be via a formal funding panel. The documentation that is required to make an application will vary from locality to locality, and as with the local thresholds and definitions considered within this chapter you should make sure that you use the required forms, reports and templates when undertaking your assessment.

Good Practice Point:
Paperwork Requirements

Familiarise yourself with your local area documents, templates and other requirements before completing your assessment.

Physical health often receives dominance in social care funding support with physical disability and older people constituting the majority group. This does not mean that other groups of individuals do not have eligible needs, but it can be more difficult to demonstrate within an assessment process.

The remainder of this chapter considers the domains within FACS that apply to psychosocial needs, and explores how these are applied to ensure that a personalised approach is taken and individuals are able to access the range of support options that may be available to them via the social care system.

DOMAIN: HEALTH AND SAFETY

Health and safety is linked to the following outcomes detailed in *Our Health, Our Care, Our Say* (DOH 2006), and social workers need to consider whether the individual's needs prevent the achievement of the outcomes (DOH 2010a) as part of their professional assessments:

- Health and well-being, including mental and emotional as well as physical health and well-being.
- Freedom from harm, abuse and neglect, taking wider issues of housing and community safety into account.

The advent of personalisation, and the revision of the FACS framework to reflect the agenda, have necessitated guidance which states that:

> with the exception of life-threatening circumstances or where there are serious safeguarding concerns, there is no hierarchy of needs . . . needs relating to social inclusion and participation should be seen as just as important as needs relating to personal care issues, where the need falls within the same band.

> (DOH 2010a: 23)

Health and safety issues are only applicable to critical and substantial bandings, and thus in most instances where a health or safety issue is identified, it is likely to be an eligible need. The complexity arises in the link between health and safety concerns and psychosocial needs, and it can be difficult for social workers to identify a clear link between, for example, social inclusion and critical health and safety issues. Table 2.1 provides an overview of the FACS criteria that apply in this domain and provides examples of how this may be applied to psychosocial needs.

Table 2.1 Health and safety FACS criteria with practice examples

	Critical	Substantial
FACS criteria	Life is, or will be threatened Significant health problems have or will develop Serious abuse or neglect has occurred or will occur	Abuse or neglect has occurred or will occur
Practice example	Serious abuse is occurring and the person's life/health is at immediate risk, for example, the person is being physically abused by their informal carer but is remaining in the abusive situation as they believe they have nowhere else to go	Self-neglect is occurring that is leading to significant social problems, for example, personal hygiene has deteriorated to such a point that the person is experiencing exclusion for their local community

It may be that in cases of mental health issues, the use of the Mental Health Act is a more appropriate option, particularly where the person meets the specified criteria of suffering from a mental disorder to a nature or degree that warrants assessment or treatment in hospital for the purposes of the individual's health, safety or protection of others (Mental Health Act 1983, as amended 2007). This may also be the case in instances where the individual lacks capacity and requires 'acts in connection with care or treatment' (Mental Capacity Act 2005, Section 5) which may be better provided under the Mental Capacity Act 2005.

It is important that social workers are aware of all the options available to meet the individual's presenting needs, and the option to access social care support in response to a risky situation, where this is a more appropriate option, should be one of the considerations you make within your assessment.

Example from Practice

Sharon was a 33-year-old woman with a long history of mental health issues and contact with the criminal justice system. She was considered to have a borderline personality disorder and had an IQ of 69. Sharon was well known by local services and was regularly picked up by the community police team for soliciting. She had been assaulted numerous times and presented to A&E on a regular basis as a result of self-harming behaviour (cutting arms and thighs).

One evening Sharon was picked up by the police after being found wandering in the street, she was covered in blood from numerous superficial cuts and had a black eye and broken nose, which she reported had happened earlier that day when a group of young men had assaulted her on her way home through the park.

Sharon was referred to the vulnerable adults team, and the assessing social worker believed that Sharon had capacity in relation to her treatment and her account of the incident, and there was no evidence to support a mental health assessment. However, Sharon was clearly vulnerable and her health and safety were presenting a risk to her continuing independence. As a result, a full community care assessment was carried out.

Sharon's assessed needs included:

- Awareness of danger/hazards and the ability to keep herself safe.
- She was unable to manage her money and was engaging in risky behaviour to obtain finances.
- She was socially isolated and sought companionship from strangers which was placing her safety at risk.
- Sharon was clear that she wanted to remain in her current flat, however, she was aware that she was not managing as well as she could and described often being scared at home alone.

Plan

Sharon's needs were assessed as eligible within the substantial banding because abuse and neglect have occurred, and the likelihood of reoccurrence was significant without intervention.

Sharon was allocated a personal budget and supported to access budgeting support from her local welfare advisor. She used her personal budget to fund transport and fees to access a local community education programme where she was able to socialise with others in a safe environment. As a result, the risks to Sharon's independence due to the identified health and safety issues were addressed and her overall well-being began to improve.

Commentary

The above case provides just one example of the types of intervention that can be applied to enable service users to access appropriate social care support. Health and safety issues are not just a result of physical impairment, and the individual's psychological and social needs can be just as risky in terms of the person's well-being. In Sharon's case, her lack of awareness of danger, combined with her social isolation which led her to making poor choices, constitutes a direct correlation between psychosocial needs and eligibility against FACS, which can be applied to a personalised approach.

> ### Reminder Checklist: Health and Safety Domain
>
> ✓ Have you considered any safeguarding issues and how these may impact upon the person's eligibility under the Health and Safety domain?
>
> ✓ Have you considered the impact of the person's ability to self-safeguard and self-protect and how this can be supported/maximised?
>
> ✓ Have you considered the individual's wider social context and any health and safety risks that may arise from this?
>
> ✓ Have you focused on the risks to independence and clearly set out how health and safety impacts upon this?
>
> ✓ Have you considered which informal supports or community options may be available to support the individual and, where this is not appropriate, identified the reasons?

DOMAIN: PERSONAL AND DAILY ROUTINES

Personal and daily routines include a range of activities including personal care and domestic tasks. This is not clearly defined within the FACS guidance (DOH 2003; DOH 2010a) but rather is open to interpretation by local authorities. Some authorities clearly state what they consider to be vital, while others assess this on a case-by-case basis.

Unlike the Health and Safety domain, personal and daily tasks are considered in all four bands (Table 2.2), and it may be that some tasks are not eligible for support from local authorities. This can be in

Table 2.2 Personal and daily routines FACS criteria with practice examples

	Critical	Substantial	Moderate	Low
FACS criteria	There is, or will be, an inability to carry out vital personal care or domestic routines	There is, or will be, an inability to carry out the majority of personal care or domestic routines	There is, or will be, an inability to carry out several personal care or domestic routines	There is, or will be, an inability to carry out one or two personal care or domestic routines
Practice example	The individual is unable to administer their own medication, for example, a person's cognitive impairment means they repeatedly forget to take medication and they deteriorate to the point of severe self-harm	The individual is unable to dress themselves appropriately, for example, a person's delusional beliefs or lack of orientation make them unable to identify which clothing is appropriate for the weather and/or environment	The individual is unable to provide themselves with a hot meal, for example, a person's mental health impacts upon their motivation and life skills which means they cannot cook but they are able to make a cold snack or drink	The individual can manage medication but only with the aid of a blister pack, for example, the person routinely forgets what medication they need to take but can self-medicate if their tablets are set out by day/time

conflict with the aims of personalisation, which promote individual choice and aspiration, and where authorities have set out what they consider to be vital, the impact on the individual of their ability (or inability) to undertake the said task is often not considered.

The concept of 'vital' tasks can be a complex one which is based upon personal values. Where one person may view the ability to have a bath or shower every day or week as essential, another person may not. The general rule of thumb is that a task is vital if it would be considered so by the majority of the local population. However, there is also a tendency by local authorities to consider vital and essential in terms of what is necessary for health, safety and hygiene rather than in terms of quality of life and individual well-being.

Good Practice Point: Vital Tasks

Make sure you know what your authority classes as vital before undertaking your assessment. Your local policies should clearly set this out.

Table 2.3 provides an overview of some of the definitions that are included in Local Authority FACS policies, you will need to check your Local Authority policies to make sure you are clear about what is considered a vital personal or daily routine in your locality, however, these examples provide an overview of the types of activities included in local definitions.

While there are common themes in relation to personal hygiene and toileting, one of the key area that you will need to consider when undertaking an eligibility assessment is the psychosocial impact on the individual of being unable to undertake personal care and daily routines.

Table 2.3 Overview of selected definitions included in Local Authority FACS policies

	Hertfordshire County Council (2003)	Croydon Social Services (n.d.)	City of York Council (2011)
Personal routine	Getting in and out of bed safely	Purchase and/or preparation of food and drinks	Getting in and out of bed each day
	Up and down from a chair safely	Eating and drinking	Transfer between bed and chair each day
	Washing whole body	Using the toilet and continence management (including associated laundry)	Have prepared food and drink in keeping with religious and cultural beliefs
	Dressing and undressing		
	Using toilet or otherwise manage continence	Routine catheter and stoma care	Wash your hands and face daily
	Eating and drinking	Essential personal hygiene (e.g. being able to wash once a day)	Wash all over weekly or as necessary to maintain personal hygiene
	Manage medication safely	Essential transfers/mobility within the home (including getting up and going to bed)	Looking after your body (e.g. teeth, nails)
		Dressing and undressing	Having access to toilet facilities
			Have toileting arrangements that are hygienic and without risk to health

Daily routine	Obtaining suitably prepared food	Assistance with orientation or motivation	Have clean outer clothing at least weekly
	Maintain a minimum safe level of hygiene in the house, including essential laundry	Essential financial management	Have clean bed linen at least fortnightly
	Summon assistance in an emergency	Essential household hygiene	Have correct benefit entitlements
		Claim welfare benefits	Pay essential bills

Good Practice Point: Psychosocial Impact of Routines

Make sure you consider the psychosocial impacts of personal and daily routines – it may be that the impact of the inability to undertake the task has a greater impact than the task itself.

Example from Practice

Harry is 43 years old and has a diagnosis of schizophrenia. He has been in and out of hospital since his early twenties, and has limited social and daily living skills. Following a recent admission under Section 3 of the Mental Health Act (for treatment), he has been discharged with an after-care package under Section 117 of the Mental Health Act. Harry's ability to self-care is very dependent on his mood and levels of motivation, and he struggles to maintain a regular routine.

Harry's care coordinator undertook a community care assessment prior to his hospital discharge, and identified the following needs in relation to personal care and daily routines:

■ Regularly forgetting medication which may result in relapse in mental state.
■ Harry's condition results in low motivation which impacts on ability to undertake personal hygiene tasks.
■ Sporadic eating patterns due to forgetfulness and motivation – will go for up to a week without a hot meal which is impacting upon Harry's health.

Plan

Harry's needs are assessed as eligible under the substantial criteria and in his Local Authority area this means he is entitled to social care support. His needs are not considered critical as they are not currently life-threatening, and he is able to maintain a low level of personal care and nutrition which means he is not considered to be in an immediate risk situation. However, as these areas impact upon his health and well-being, the assessment indicates that there is a direct link between his mental health issues and his ability to self-care, and thus substantial criteria are applied in relation to these needs.

His personal support plan states that he requires support in relation to medication, personal care and nutrition; however, he is clear that he wants to be independent and does not want a home carer; he believes that as he is physically able to undertake tasks, he does not need a carer.

- Telecare equipment is provided to prompt Harry to take his medication as prescribed and the local chemist provides this in weekly blister packs to ensure that he knows which medication he needs to take when the telecare prompt is received.
- Harry is supported by his care coordinator to access a local lunch club twice a week and direct payments are established to fund his place at the club and his transport to the appropriate venue. This is a community group in his local area, and through this contact Harry is also able to participate in cooking classes to increase his awareness of the importance of nutrition and its impact on his psychological needs. It also provides Harry with activity and social contact which are also identified as substantial needs within the assessment process.
- Harry's involvement in the lunch club supports improvement in his personal care as he is able to establish a routine of showering prior to attending the group.

Commentary

The Example from practice provided highlights the issue of the impact that personal care and daily routines can have on a person's well-being. When considering the psychosocial needs of an individual, it is important to consider their emotional welfare in terms of how the inability to self-care can affect them. This dimension has the potential to create significant difficulties for the individual and a personalised approach needs to ensure that the whole person is considered in any assessment and identification of needs. In Harry's case, his eligible needs are intertwined with his mental health condition, and supporting access to one activity to meet his nutritional needs also has the potential to have a positive impact on his wider social needs by creating a routine and identifying the potential social barriers he may face as a result of poor personal hygiene.

Good Practice Point: Linking Support Options

Remember that support mechanisms to support individuals to address one area of need may positively impact on a different need. No support option should be viewed in isolation, and social workers will need to be aware of the wider impacts and implications of any social care support provided. This should be considered within the wider personalised support planning process to promote a whole-person view of any plans that are agreed with the service user and/or carer.

Reminder Checklist: Daily and Personal Routines Domain

✓ Have you considered the individual's wider social context and any daily and personal routines that may present a risk to this?

✓ Have you included an analysis of the routines the person is able to undertake and how these are supported/sustained?

✓ Have you focused on the risks to independence and clearly set out how the person's needs within their daily and personal routines may impact upon this?

✓ Have you considered which informal sports or community options may be available to support the individual and, where this is not appropriate, identified the reasons?

DOMAIN: FAMILY AND COMMUNITY LIFE

Unlike the Health and Safety and Personal Care domains of FACS, the Family and Community Life domain is not as clear-cut in terms of what is considered the 'normal' level of family and community involvement. Views will vary based on personal values and experience, and the social worker will need to be able to identify their own values and beliefs in relation to this area to ensure that the individual's understanding and relationship aspirations remain central to the assessment process.

Table 2.4 provides an overview of the FACS bandings in relation to family and social life and presents an example of how these can be interpreted.

Cultural views and norms will need to be considered within this domain. Family roles can vary, and the individual should be supported to maintain these relationships as they can potentially improve an individual's well-being and quality of life. As with the personal care domain, what is considered a vital family role or relationship can be open to interpretation, and the practitioner will need to consider the psychosocial impacts of roles and relationships, including the impact on the person if these are not sustained. In many cases, informal care and support is a vital mechanism, and without family and carers, the individual would be less likely to maintain, or improve on their level of independence.

Carers are also entitled to assessment and support from LSSAs where their needs are assessed as eligible, and social workers should be aware of both sets of criteria (including the ways they can potentially interact) in order to comprehensively assess an individual's needs and circumstances under the FACS criteria and in relation to the social care outcomes set out in both the White Paper *Our Health, Our Care, Our Say* (DOH 2006) and reinforced in the *Putting People First* concordat (HM Government 2007).

Table 2.4 Overview of the FACS bandings in relation to family and social life with practice examples

	Critical	Substantial	Moderate	Low
FACS criteria	Vital support systems and relationships cannot or will not be sustained Vital family and other social roles and responsibilities cannot or will not be undertaken Vital involvement in work, education or learning cannot or will not be sustained	The majority of social support systems and relationships cannot or will not be sustained The majority of family and other social roles and responsibilities cannot or will not be undertaken Involvement in many aspects of work, education or learning cannot or will not be sustained	Several support systems and relationships cannot or will not be sustained Several family or other social roles and responsibilities cannot or will not be undertaken Involvement in several aspects of work, education or learning cannot or will not be sustained	One or two social support systems and relationships cannot or will not be sustained One or two family and other social roles and responsibilities cannot or will not be undertaken Involvement in one or two aspects of work, education or learning cannot or will not be sustained
Practice example	The relationship with carer/s is in danger of breaking down, for example, a person is in regular conflict with their carer due to delusional beliefs that they are trying to harm them which is leading to aggression and personal safety issues	The individual has no one to turn to in emergency situation, for example, the person is estranged from family and has no friends to rely on if they are unable to cope at home on their own	Support is needed to engage in occupational activities which would help to prevent relapse, for example, a person's anxiety prevents them from accessing community activities	Someone who would prefer to live closer to family members, for example, a person lives many miles from family and has lost their driving licence due to the prescribed medication they need to take to maintain their mental health

Good Practice Point: Social Context

Social workers should ensure they are familiar with both service user and carer eligibility criteria within their local authority area. Remember that a person-centred assessment should consider the person within their social context, promoting involvement and participation often has a positive impact on other FACS domains and the individual's overall well-being.

As is the case in other FACS domains, what is determined to be vital will vary according to local area, and authorities will need to consider what they believe to be such roles and responsibilities. Parenting, caring and spousal relationships are likely to be considered to be vital, however, other roles and relationships will be interpreted by the authority and social workers may find that different rules apply in different areas.

Example from Practice

Lauren and James have been married 10 years and have three children aged between 3 and 10 years old. Lauren's mother also lives with them and the whole family support her as she is increasingly frail and confused, with a diagnosis of vascular dementia. James works full-time as a salesman and Lauren stays at home with her children and mother. She is the main carer as James has limited time off work and his income supports the family. Lauren herself has had periods of depression in the past and has been supported on and off by her local mental health team. Over the past year Lauren has found things particularly difficult, and has begun to experience some obsessive compulsive symptoms in addition to her depression. The supporting team are aware of this and believe that stress and the demands of looking after her children and her mother are contributing to her declining mental health.

A re-assessment was carried out with Lauren and her family and, as a result of the impact of her caring roles, which were considered vital, on her mental health and general well-being, she was assessed as having eligible needs under FACS within this domain. The view was taken that her needs were critical as Lauren would potentially be unable to undertake vital roles without additional support.

Outcome

Lauren did not wish to give up her roles and was reluctant to accept carer input, however, she recognised that without some support, her own health and well-being were at risk and this in turn impacted on her ability to manage her roles and responsibilities in relation to the needs of her family. Lauren's needs were assessed as eligible and a personal budget was agreed with a support plan which included regular scheduled time-outs for Lauren when additional support would be provided to her mother. Lauren was able to join a local arts class and fund her transport and materials which gave her the break she needed.

Commentary

In the case of Lauren and her family, a range of needs are evident within the family context and these may each be eligible under FACS for social care support. While her mother may be eligible for support in her own right, in this instance Lauren's needs take precedence as she provides significant informal support which enables her mother to remain at home. If this role were to break down, the impact would be detrimental to Lauren's independence as it is a vital role which provides purpose, structure and routine as well as contributing to Lauren's sense of identity and self-worth. She is very keen to maintain the current situation and becomes very distressed if formal care is suggested and thus the focus in this instance is on the impact of her being unable to undertake her roles and the risks this would present to Lauren's well-being.

Reminder Checklist: Family and Community Life

✓ Have you considered the individual's wider social context and any daily and personal routines that may present a risk to this?

✓ Have you included an analysis of the routines the person is able to undertake and how these are supported/sustained?

✓ Have you focused on the risks to independence and clearly set out how the person's needs within their daily and personal routines may impact upon this?

✓ Have you considered what informal supports or community options may be available to support the individual and, where this is not appropriate, identified the reasons?

DOMAIN: AUTONOMY AND CHOICE

The fourth domain within the FACS framework relates to an individual's level of autonomy and control over their own lives. This is an area that is particularly relevant within the context of personalisation, an approach which places individual choice and control as one of its central elements. The evidence base indicates that increased ownership results in better outcomes (Langan and Lidlow 2004; DOH 2007). However, this is not always easy to apply in terms of assessment of eligible needs, and as with the family and community life domain, workers will need to provide an analysis and rationale for the causal link between their safety and well-being and the level of autonomy exercised by the individual.

Table 2.5 sets out the FACS criteria within this domain and provides an example of this practice. As with the Health and Safety domain, there is no guidance for moderate and low bandings in this area, and

Table 2.5 Autonomy and choice FACS criteria with practice examples

	Critical	Substantial
FACS criteria	There is, or will be, little or no choice and control over vital aspects of the immediate environment	There is, or will be, only partial choice and control over the immediate environment
Practice example	The individual's mental health condition is unable to make any choices or exercise control as a direct result of their condition, for example, an individual who is experiencing acute psychosis may be unable to make choices and/or decisions and others may be required to act in their best interests in most instances	The individual's mental health condition fluctuates and impacts on their ability to make choices, for example, a person with severe anxiety may be unable to exercise a number of choices/or has limited choices in their lives but the severity of this varies according to how mentally well they are at any given point in time

thus where an individual is assessed as lacking autonomy or experiencing restricted choices, these are likely to be either critical/substantial, or issues that the authority disregards in terms of entitlements to support.

Good Practice Point: Choice and Control

Choice and control are key themes in a personalised approach to social care. All your activities from assessment for eligibility through to ongoing support planning and reviews should consider the service user and carer involvement with a view to maximising individual choice and control.

Example from Practice

Steve experiences periods of psychosis during which time he is unable to make decisions about his home and living arrangements, including aspects such as making sure his bills are paid, buying food and topping up his gas and electricity meters.

Steve and his worker have agreed a crisis and contingency plan for these times and it has been identified that Steve needs some support to make arrangements that can be activated if he becomes unwell – this includes contacting his bank, the Department of Work and Pensions and his gas and electricity providers to establish action plans to make sure his decisions and choices are sustained at times when additional support is needed.

Outcome

As Steve is assessed as having substantial needs in this domain, he is able to access social care support. His worker and his informal network are able to support some of his needs, and his local citizens advice service provides additional support to negotiate with his various providers and his landlord to set up arrangements that can be maintained electronically and alerts are set up to inform Steve's mother should he alter these arrangements.

Steve's eating patterns can be sporadic and this is a sign that his mental health is deteriorating, so an arrangement is agreed with the local service broker so that Steve is able to activate a personal assistant to support him with shopping and household chores when needed – this has an impact on Steve's well-being and supports his autonomy and choices as well as promoting his ability to maintain his personal and daily routines. A notional personal budget is allocated for this service which Steve's worker is able to agree up to an approved limit which minimises the delay in being able to start and end the service as per Steve's fluctuating needs.

Commentary

By planning ahead and identifying creative options to manage his affairs and choices if he becomes unwell, Steve has effectively developed a plan which means he is able to maintain his autonomy and choices even at times when he would be considered to lack capacity to manage his situation. While some of Steve's needs are clearly a health concern and relate directly to the impact of his mental health, he has a range of social care needs, which can be supported in a personalised way. These needs are assessed as substantial, and as such Steve would be eligible for support.

Supporting independence means that when Steve is able to manage his own situation, his support plan needs to change to promote this. However, a rapid change may be needed to increase support when it is required. A personalised approach to social care enables this to happen by establishing triggers and plans with Steve, and ensuring his autonomy and choice are maximised to sustain and improve his current level of independence.

Reminder Checklist: Autonomy and Choice Domain

✓ Have you considered the individual's wider social context and any risks that are presented relating to the availability of opportunities and choices?

✓ Have you focused on the risks to independence and clearly set out how the person's needs, wishes and aspirations, including the level of control a person has in their daily life may impact upon this?

✓ Have you considered which informal supports or community options may be available to support the individual and, where this is not appropriate, identified the reasons why?

SUMMARY

This chapter has considered the four domains within the FACS criteria in relation to psychosocial needs and has placed this within a personalised support approach. Workers should remember that other needs in relation to physical health or conditions may be relevant when working with particular individuals and thus the whole personal circumstances of each individual and their context need to be considered as part of the assessment process.

Eligibility under FACS does allow for personalised needs to be supported. However, in times of austerity it becomes increasingly important for social workers undertaking the assessment and funding application (where relevant) to fully analyse and explore the full range of needs, strengths and resources and how these can impact upon an individual's well-being and independence. Informal support networks must be accessed within any support planning process, and the needs of carers and family units should be included in the assessment wherever relevant. Your Local Authority will have its own policies and procedures and these should always be followed, and it is useful to make sure you are aware of how local and national policy approaches are linked.

This chapter is designed to assist you to think about how you undertake FACS eligibility assessments and consider some of the issues that may arise in terms of applying the framework. It is not intended to be an exclusive review but rather to provide guidance to help you to reflect upon and develop your own practice, and provide an overview/quick reference to the criteria and how they are applied.

Good Practice Point: Think About Prevention

Remember that your assessment should not just consider immediate needs but also should take a longer-term preventative view. For example, a current need may not appear to be 'critical' at the time of the assessment but, by not providing some level of support now, this might mean the problem becomes much bigger at a later stage.

Reminder Checklist: Applying FACS

✓ Have you focused on the risks to independence and clearly set out how the person's needs within each domain impact upon this?

✓ Have you considered what informal supports or community options may be available to support the individual and, where this is not appropriate, identified the reasons why?

✓ Have you reviewed your authority's thresholds and criteria and applied your assessment to this framework?

✓ Have you analysed your assessment, ensuring that you demonstrate how needs and strengths interact?

✓ Have you considered all of the FACS domains and the individual's whole personal circumstances?

✓ Have you undertaken an analysis to identify where needs impact upon each other?

✓ Have you reflected the individual's wishes and aspirations throughout the assessment?

3 **NHS Continuing Healthcare**

The separation of health and social care needs is not clear-cut, and social workers will need an awareness of the complex systems that are in place to access funding and services for individuals beyond those of the Local Authority Fair Access to Care eligibility. In addition to accessing funds via social care, practitioners will need to ensure that continuing care is considered, and this includes consideration of a separate set of criteria and eligibility.

Similar to Chapter 2, this chapter sets out the requirements of NHS Continuing Healthcare, and encourages practitioners to consider whether this framework has the potential to provide additional options in terms of maximising service users' support choices and outcomes.

DEFINING THE TERMS

Continuing care and continuing healthcare are terms that are often used interchangeably, however, they do refer to different elements of care, and as such it is useful to be clear about which you are referring to.

The term 'continuing care' in policy means 'care provided over an extended period of time, to a person aged 18 or over, to meet physical or mental health needs that have arisen as a result of disability, accident or illness' (DOH 2009a: 4).

NHS Continuing Healthcare is a package of continuing care that is arranged and funded solely by the NHS for those individuals whose healthcare needs require ongoing support and/or treatment.

Good Practice Point: Clarity of Term

Make sure you are clear about which term you are using and its context. An individual may have continuing care needs which are neither a primary health need nor eligible for NHS funding, and thus you need to be clear what you are referring to, especially when providing information and advice for service users and carers.

The current framework for NHS Continuing Healthcare was published in 2009, and Directions were issued under the National Health Service Act 2006 and the Local Authority Social Services Act 1970 (DOH 2009c) to support the revised framework.

Point of Law: NHS Continuing Healthcare (Responsibilities) Directions 2009

(2) . . . a Primary Care Trust must take reasonable steps to ensure that an assessment of eligibility for NHS Continuing Healthcare is carried out in all cases where it appears to the Trust that –

(a) there may be a need for such care; or

(b) an individual who is receiving NHS Continuing Healthcare may no longer be eligible for such care.

The duties of the Primary Care Trust (PCT) under these Directions are very similar to the duty to assess requirements for local authorities under Section 47 of the NHS and Community Care Act 1990. As with Section 47(3) of the earlier piece of legislation, the NHS Continuing Healthcare (Responsibilities) Directions 2009 place a requirement to cooperate and consult on both PCTs and LAs, aiming to create an integrated approach where an individual may have continuing care needs that span both health and social care frameworks.

Good Practice Point: Contact the PCT

Make sure you have considered your responsibilities in terms of making contact with your local PCT where you identify as part of your assessment that there may be primary health needs that should be assessed.

Eligibility for NHS Continuing Healthcare (CHC) has been subject to several court judgments and subsequent case law, which led up to the review and revisions published in 2009. Two of these are of particular significance: *R v North and East Devon Health Authority, ex parte Pamela Coughlan* (known as the Coughlan judgment) and *R v Bexley NHS Care Trust, ex parte Grogan* (known as the Grogan judgment). These two cases were specifically considering the eligibility criteria for continuing healthcare, and included the responsibilities of both health authorities and local authorities in meeting individual needs in each case (see DOH 2009a, for more information on these judgments).

As with the term 'continuing care', the term 'primary health need' does not appear in primary legislation, but does feature heavily in the policy, guidance and directions that support the operation and delivery of NHS Continuing Healthcare. Determining whether someone has a primary health need involves the consideration of a number of areas, including whether the nursing or health services are no more than incidental or ancillary to the accommodation LAs would be required to provide or whether they are of a nature beyond those for which the LA would be expected to have responsibility.

In addition to the considerations in relation to which authority may be responsible for individual needs, the National Framework sets out four characteristics that should be explored when determining whether an individual could be classed as having a primary health need. These are:

- *Nature*: The particular characteristics of the need and the effect of those needs on the individual, including the type of interventions needed to manage them.
- *Intensity*: The extent and severity of the needs and the support needed to meet them, including the need for ongoing care.
- *Complexity*: How the needs present and interact, and the level of skill needed to monitor, treat and/or manage the care. There may be single or multiple conditions or interactions, and assessment includes the individual's response to their situation where this impacts on the needs.
- *Unpredictability*: The degree to which needs fluctuate and hence create management challenges. This includes the level of risk to the person's health if care is not provided appropriately and in a timely manner (DOH 2009a: 10).

Reminder Checklist: 'Health Needs' Characteristics

Nature

- ✓ Does the individual describe their needs in health terms?
- ✓ What impact do their needs have on their overall health and well-being?
- ✓ Do the needs require a skilled/trained response?
- ✓ What would happen if these needs were not met? Or not met in a timely way?

Intensity

- ✓ How severe is the need?
- ✓ How often and for how long is intervention needed?

✓ How many carers/workers will be required to meet the need?
✓ Does the care needed cover more than one domain?

Complexity

✓ How difficult is it to manage the needs?
✓ Are needs interrelated or do they impact on each other to increase the difficulty in meeting needs?
✓ Do the needs require a skilled/trained response?
✓ Does the person's response to their needs impact on the ability to meet the needs?

Unpredictability

✓ Is the person's condition stable/deteriorating/improving?
✓ Is the person or their carer able to anticipate when needs might arise?
✓ Does the level of need often change or require support to be frequently altered to meet needs?
✓ How significant are the consequences if a need is not addressed when it arises?

Adapted from (DOH 2010b: 23–4)

The above checklist has been constructed to help you think about your practice and individual cases. It is not a comprehensive screening tool and further assessment will be needed, including potentially completing the CHC checklist and decision support tool (DST) alongside any other local procedures. However, it will help you to consider whether the individual may have a health need that could require continuing care of some degree or description. These characteristics, either alone or in combination, may indicate that the individual has a primary health need, and this will be because of the quality or quantity of care required to meet the individual's needs (DOH 2009d), and thus it is important that you are clear about the individual's possible eligibility to make sure the individual has access to all service and funding options needed to maximise their overall well-being and quality of life.

NHS CONTINUING HEALTHCARE ELIGIBILITY FRAMEWORK

The level of complexity, whether the need is considered to be a 'primary health need' and whether care is required beyond that which a local authority would be expected to provide, are all issues that need to be considered in the assessment process and whether social workers undertake the assessment or the task is the responsibility of a specific professional, it is useful to be able to consider whether continuing healthcare is a potential option.

An individual will be eligible for NHS continuing healthcare where it can be said that their 'primary need is a health need'. The decision as to whether a person has a primary health need takes into account the legal limits of Local Authority (LA) provision.

(DOH 2009d: 2)

Point of Policy: NHS Continuing Healthcare Eligibility

The reasons given for a decision on eligibility should NOT be based on:

(i)   The person's diagnosis.
(ii) The care setting.
(iii) The ability of the provider to manage care.
(iv) The use (or not) of NHS-employed staff to provide care.
(v)   The need for/presence of 'specialist staff' in care delivery.

(vi) The fact a need is well managed.
(vii) The existence of other NHS funded care; or
(viii) Any other input-related rationale.

(DOH 2009a: 15)

In order to be eligible for NHS Continuing Healthcare, the individual needs to meet a set of criteria in relation to a range of 12 healthcare need domains:

- *Behaviour*
- *Cognition*
- *Psychological/Emotional*
- Communication
- Mobility
- Nutrition
- Continence
- Skin integrity
- Breathing
- *Drug therapies, medications and symptom control*
- Altered states of consciousness

(DOH 2009b)

Those highlighted in the above list will be considered in detail in this volume to support decisions in practice. Those domains relating to physical healthcare needs in the list above are not discussed here as the purpose of this book is to apply eligibility criteria to psychosocial needs. However, it may be that these are relevant in cases where individuals have a range of both physical and mental health needs, and thus social workers should familiarise themselves with the criteria in these areas as appropriate (see DOH 2009a; 2009b; 2009d, for full information and guidance on all domains).

Good Practice Point: Consider the Whole Picture

Remember that individuals usually have more than one need, and the person's whole circumstances and expectations should be considered.

SCREENING FOR NHS CONTINUING HEALTHCARE

When undertaking screening to determine whether an individual has a primary health need in any of the NHS Continuing Healthcare (CHC) domains, the characteristics should be applied to determine the intensity, complexity and unpredictability of any given need. The Department of Health Checklist is designed to provide a screening tool for practitioners considering appropriate care and support options for health needs, and additional decision support tools are also available for download from the Department of Health web pages (www.dh.gov.uk), accessible by searching 'NHS Continuing Healthcare'.

Good Practice Point: The NHS Framework and Local Policies

Make sure you are familiar with both the National Framework for NHS Continuing Healthcare and your local PCT policies, including referral routes and assessment processes where appropriate. This will help you to consider all the possible options for the individuals whom you are assessing and may assist you to access additional support packages and options.

Within the eligibility framework, needs are categorised into several levels: no need (N), low (L), moderate (M), high (H), severe (S) and priority (P). Figure 3.1 illustrates the levels available in each of the various domains.

Figure 3.1 NHS Continuing Healthcare domain levels

Domain	P	S	H	M	L	N
Behaviour	P	S	H	M	L	N
Cognition		S	H	M	L	N
Psychological/ Emotional			H	M	L	N
Communication			H	M	L	N
Mobility		S	H	M	L	N
Nutrition		S	H	M	L	N
Continence			H	M	L	N
Skin and Tissue Viability		S	H	M	L	N
Breathing	P	S	H	M	L	N
Drug Therapies	P	S	H	M	L	N
Altered States of Consciousness	P		H	M	L	N
Other Significant Care Needs		S	H	M	L	N

Note: Those highlighted will be explored in more detail to assist social workers in applying the criteria to individuals' psychosocial needs.

Source: (DOH 2009d: 6).

**Good Practice Point:
A Holistic Approach**

Individuals rarely have only one need – make sure you take a
holistic approach to all your assessment practices and
consider the interactions and impacts of each of the person's
presenting needs and strengths.

The practice guidance published by the Department of Health (DOH
2010b) states:

> An individual has a primary health need if, having taken account of
> all their needs ... it can be said that the main aspects or majority
> part of the care they require is focused on addressing and/or
> preventing health needs.

(DOH 2010b: 22)

As such, in order for a need to be considered a primary health need,
and to be eligible for continuing healthcare funding, the assessment is
expected to show that:

- A level of 'priority' is indicated in any one of the four domains
  that carry this level.
- Two or more of the identified severe needs exist across all care
  domains (DOH 2009d: 9).

In some cases, a primary health need may also be indicated if:

- One domain is identified as severe and there are needs in a
  number of other domains.
- A number of domains are indicated as high and/or moderate
  (DOH 2009d: 9).

Therefore, it is useful for practitioners to understand how the criteria are
applied and to consider these within their assessment processes to ensure
all the options are considered in relation to meeting individuals' needs.

Reminder Checklist: When Should NHS Continuing Healthcare be Considered?

✓ As part of your community care assessment.
✓ When support packages or placements are reviewed.
✓ When medical/nursing reviews are carried out.
✓ Where there have been repeated and regular changes to individual needs.
✓ In any other circumstances that suggest the person has a primary health need and may be eligible for NHS Continuing Healthcare.

The remainder of this chapter will consider those domains which relate to psychosocial and complex needs in detail, to assist social workers to consider how these can be applied to psychosocial and complex needs, and how this can be used to maximise a personalised approach which emphasises independence and well-being.

Good Practice Point: Know the CHC Policy

Make sure you are familiar with your local area's CHC policy and guidance as well as being aware of the national requirements. As with FACS, local areas will have systems and procedures in place that you will need to navigate.

DOMAIN: BEHAVIOUR

Challenging behaviour is a term usually used within health and social care to describe behaviour that presents a risk to the individual or others, or is difficult to manage within services. It is often used to describe aggression and violence, however, that is a narrow definition and social workers will need to consider the impact of an individual's behaviour both in terms of health and safety for the social worker, and also on services, in terms of the way behaviour is managed within a service context.

It is difficult to identify specific behaviours that may be included within this domain, and social workers will need to assess and consider each case individually. However, the CHC decision support tool (DOH 2009d) provides some examples and includes the following:

- Aggression, violence and passive-aggressive behaviour.
- Severe disinhibition or inappropriate interference with others.
- Consistent nosiness or restlessness, or extreme frustration.
- Severe fluctuations in mental state.
- Resistance to care and/or treatment.
- High risk of suicide.

(DOH 2009d: 15)

As a social worker assessing an individual and considering the possible eligibility of individuals for CHC, you will need to ensure that you fully consider both the presenting behaviour and its impact upon the individual, their circumstances, other people and the provision of services. It is not sufficient to simply identify the behaviour, you will also need to be clear about the evidence that the behaviour is, first, occurring as a result of a primary health need (see Reminder Checklist: 'Health Needs' Characteristics on p. 49), and, second, is having a significant impact on the person's health and well-being.

Table 3.1 sets out the DOH guidance in relation to the nature, intensity, complexity and predictability of an individual's presentation and needs within this domain and provides some practical examples of what might be included in each level. This is not intended as an exclusive list, but rather to provide a basis for social workers to start thinking about whether CHC may be an appropriate avenue to explore.

Table 3.1 Department of Health guidance in relation to the nature, intensity, complexity and predictability of an individual's presentation and needs (domain: behaviour)

Level	Description	Example
No need	No evidence of challenging behaviour	
Low	Some incidents of challenging behaviour Risk assessment indicates behaviour does not pose a risk to self or others or a barrier to intervention The person is compliant with all aspects of their care	A person occasionally becomes frustrated as they feel out of control of their health issues This can result in irritability and hostile responses to those attempting to provide treatment and/or support
Moderate	Challenging behaviour follows a predictable pattern Risk assessment indicates a pattern of behaviour which can be managed by skilled carers or workers who can maintain a level of behaviour that does not pose a risk to self or others The person is nearly always compliant with care	A person becomes highly agitated at regular frequencies which are linked to family visits The agitation is responsive to de-escalation and staff are able to implement consistent strategies to minimise the distress and disruption caused by the challenging behaviour

High	Challenging behaviour that poses a predictable risk to self or others Risk assessment indicates planned interventions are effective in minimising but not always eliminating risks Compliance is variable but usually responsive to planned interventions	A person has a tendency to wander and abscond from their residence on a weekly basis during the evenings This wandering occurs as a result of disorientation and memory loss and can be managed by increased supervision during evenings
Severe	Challenging behaviour is of severity/frequency that poses significant risk to self or others Risk assessment identifies that behaviour requires a skilled and prompt responses that may be outside the range of planned interventions	A person has a fixed delusion that a neighbour is trying to harm him, this is linked directly to the person's mental health and becomes more significant during the full moon when the person repeatedly threatens the neighbour and causes damage to their garden Equipment and supervision are needed to minimise the impact of the person's behaviour in terms of both harm to the neighbour and potential repercussions of behaviour which may result in risk of harm to the person

(Continued overleaf)

Table 3.1 *Continued*

Level	Description	Example
Priority	Challenging behaviour is of severity/frequency/predictability that presents immediate and serious risk to self or others Risks are so serious that they require access to an immediate and skilled response at all times for safe care	The person has a significant history of self-harm and suicidal behaviour which is usually sustained over a period of a week at a time The person is unable or unwilling to self-manage their safety and is at continuous risk of harm, as a result, supervision and support are needed as skilled carer needs to be provided to minimise and manage the risks presented

Source: Adapted from DOH 2009d: 16.

Whether challenging behaviour is a health or social care need is a difficult determination to make and there are many areas of cross-over between CHC and FACS that may mean that there is an increased need for health and social care authorities to work together. As a result, being aware of the two frameworks and how they can interact will be helpful to decision-making in practice.

Good Practice Point: Revisit Characteristics

Revisiting the characteristics reminder box presented on p. 49 may also assist your decision-making within this domain.

Behaviour is often seen as within the control of the person and/or their carers, however, in many cases this may not be a true reflection of the person's needs and situation. Conditioned responses, based on an individual's experiences and expectations and their views, values and attitudes, may not be an informed behavioural choice. In cases such as severe mental health, dementia and learning disabilities, there may be a lack of recognition of social norms and behaviours which results in a detrimental impact on the individual whose behaviour others see as challenging. Diversity and culture will also need to be fully considered as part of the assessment of behaviour under this domain. Cultural norms shape attitudes and behaviour, and as a worker you should be aware of this possibility. You should try to source additional information about cultural and behavioural norms to inform your assessment practice.

Reminder Checklist: Behaviour Domain

✓ Have you considered and linked the individual's health issues with the subsequent behaviour and evidenced this link with specific examples/accounts?

✓ Have you illustrated the level of risk associated with the individual's behaviour?

✓ Have you considered the person's informal support networks and how these might be utilised to improve the individual's health and safety?

✓ Have you matched the person's assessed needs and presentation to the criteria set out in the CHC guidance to identify the level of need in this area against the framework?

✓ Have you considered cultural and behavioural norms and the impact of these upon the individual's presenting needs?

DOMAIN: COGNITION

Cognition refers to the individual's ability to understand and manage their daily lives. This may be in relation to confusion, orientation or memory.

Capacity should be considered as part of the CHC referral and assessment, and the DOH guidance on CHC (DOH 2009b) is very clear in its link to the five principles of the Mental Capacity Act 2005 which are summarised in the following Point of Law box.

Point of Law: Mental Capacity Act 2005 Principles

1 *Presumption of capacity*: people will be presumed to have capacity unless there is evidence to suggest otherwise.

2 *Supporting individuals to make their own decisions:* all practical steps should be taken to assist and support the person in making decisions before an assessment of incapacity is made.

3 *Best interests*: any action undertaken under the Mental Capacity Act 2005 will be carried out in the best interests of the individual.

4 *Unwise decisions*: a person should not be presumed to lack capacity just because they make decisions that others would consider to be unwise.

5 *Less restriction*: any action or decision made under the Act should consider the least amount of restriction of rights and freedoms necessary.

(Source: summarised from Section 1: MCA 2005)

Although it is linked to the capacity framework, CHC is not dependent on the individual lacking capacity, but rather considers how the individual's cognitive abilities and needs impact upon their needs in relation to both safety and daily tasks.

As with the FACS framework, it is not sufficient to just list all the information available about a person, rather, there is a real need to consider how the criteria apply in each case, and what healthcare is needed to assist the individual to manage their needs and maintain their health and independence. Conditions such as dementia, memory impairment, and other cognitive disorders which impact on the individual's ability to self-care and self-safeguard, may meet some of the criteria under this domain where the person's health and safety are affected.

Table 3.2 sets out the DOH guidance in relation to the nature, intensity, complexity and predictability of an individual's presentation and needs within this domain and provides some practical examples of what might be included in each level. This is not intended as an exhaustive list, but rather to provide a basis for social workers to start

Table 3.2   Department of Health guidance in relation to the nature, intensity, complexity and predictability of an individual's presentation and needs (domain: cognition)

Level	Description	Example
No need	No evidence of impairment, confusion or disorientation	
Low	Cognitive impairment which requires some supervision, prompting or assistance with more complex activities of daily living, and Awareness of basic risks that affect safety is evident **OR** Occasional difficulties with	A person with depression and anxiety struggles to remember where they left their keys on a regular basis and has left them in the front door a number of times The last time this happened the person was locked out of their home for

(Continued overleaf)

Table 3.2 *Continued*

Level	Description	Example
	memory and decisions which requires support, prompting or assistance, and the individual has insight into their impairment	several hours in the cold which was detrimental to their health and well-being The issue can be managed by the use of equipment (lock safe) and providing a key with the neighbour
Moderate	Cognitive impairment that requires some supervision, prompting and/or assistance with basic care needs and daily living activities Some awareness of needs and basic risks is evident The individual is usually able to make choices appropriate to needs with assistance The individual has limited ability even with supervision, prompting or assistance to make decisions about some aspects of their lives, which consequently puts them at some risk of harm, neglect or health deterioration	A person with dementia is unable to remember to take their medication on a regular basis which has an impact on treatment effectiveness and the person's well-being Supervision or equipment is needed to prompt the person to take medication at the same time each day

High	Cognitive impairment that could include marked short-term memory issues and disorientation in time and place	A person is unable to remember recent events or people involved in their life as a result of a neurological disorder
	The individual has awareness of only a limited range of needs and basic risks	They find making choices difficult and capacity in relation to making healthy choices is impaired, including regularly forgetting to eat and drink
	The person is unable to make choices on most issues even with supervision, prompting or assistance	The person needs supervision and prompting to undertake basic routines and activities and ensure that the person has adequate food and drink
	The person finds it difficult to make decisions about key aspects of life which puts them at high risk of harm, neglect or health deterioration	
Severe	Cognitive impairment which includes problems with long-term memory or severe disorientation	A person experiencing persistent psychosis is disorientated to time and place and is often unable to recognise delusion from reality, including believing that the doctors are trying to poison them which results in marked disengagement from services
	The person is unable to assess basic risks and is dependent on others to anticipate basic needs and to protect them from harm, neglect or health deterioration	

Source: Adapted from DOH 2009d: 18.

thinking about whether CHC may be an appropriate avenue to explore.

As with FACS, the key to illustrating CHC eligibility and providing evidence to support your assessment is that you will need to evidence the individual's needs, how these link to the person's overall health condition and the care needed to sustain the person's health and well-being, wherever they may reside. While hospital admission and use of the Mental Health Act and Mental Capacity Act may be appropriate in some cases, there are many individuals who live within a community setting with continuing healthcare needs.

In the case of issues such as mental health and dementia, there may be a significant overlap between healthcare and social care needs, and eligibility across both sets of eligibility criteria may need to be considered and applied.

Example from Practice

Shane has a history of mental health and substance misuse issues; he has been in and out of a range of services for many years and has served several prison sentences as a result of violence and aggression when intoxicated. Over the past few years his memory and coordination have been deteriorating and he is very frustrated and at times confused as a result. His doctors and care team suspect that he may be experiencing the onset of some type of alcohol-related dementia such as Korsakoff's syndrome, however, no firm diagnosis can be made while Shane continues to drink problematically.

Following a recent hospital admission, as a result of a head injury he sustained as a result of falling over when intoxicated, it became clear that Shane's neurological condition has progressed to the point where he is presenting as a significant risk to his own health and is unable to appreciate hazards such as road safety and domestic routines. During a community care assessment, the assessor identified that Shane potentially met the criteria for CHC and completed the standard screening tool to double check before making a formal referral for the scheme.

Commentary

In Shane's case, his health condition is deteriorating and he is experiencing significant impacts upon his health and well-being as a result. Under the CHC criteria, Shane could be assessed as having a high need in this area. This is due to the indication that safety has become a concern and he is now unable to self-safeguard, a situation which is directly attributable to his presenting health need, in this case, memory and orientation issues associated with possible dementia.

Good Practice Checklist: Cognition

✓ Have you fully considered and evidenced any capacity and best interest assessments that have been carried out?

✓ Have you fully considered and evidenced your assessment of the impact of the person's cognition on their health and safety?

✓ Have you matched the person's assessed needs and presentation to the criteria set out in the CHC guidance to identify the level of need in this area against the framework?

DOMAIN: PSYCHOLOGICAL/EMOTIONAL

Many health and well-being issues have the potential to impact upon an individual's psychological and emotional health and needs. While mental health is the central focus in this domain, it has been established that chronic difficulties with pain and physical health also have a detrimental effect on the individual's mental health and overall sense of well-being (HM Government 2011). As such, the psychosocial needs of the individual are likely to be multifaceted, and include a wide range of needs that are interdependent between the person's physical and psychological health.

Where these needs are linked to a health condition, it may be that CHC is an appropriate option to access for support and to minimise the impact of such conditions on the person's psychological and emotional state.

Table 3.3 sets out the DOH guidance in relation to the nature, intensity, complexity and predictability of an individual's presentation and needs within this domain and provides some practical examples of what might be included in each level. This is not intended as an exhaustive list, but rather to provide a basis for social workers to start thinking about whether CHC may be an appropriate avenue to explore.

Table 3.3 Department of Health guidance in relation to the nature, intensity, complexity and predictability of an individual's presentation and needs (domain: psychological/emotional)

Level	Description	Example
No need	Psychological and emotional needs are not having an impact on their health and well-being	
Low	Mood disturbance, hallucinations, anxiety or periods of distress which are having an impact on health and/or well-being but respond to prompts and reassurance	A person's mental health state means they are unable to manage their ongoing personal care needs which means their physical and mental health may be at risk but

	OR Requires prompts to motivate self towards activity and to engage in care planning, support and/or daily activities	this can be resolved by regular prompting which is responded to positively by the person and helps them to maintain their health and well-being
Moderate	Mood disturbance, hallucinations, anxiety or periods of distress which are having a severe impact on health and/or well-being which do not readily respond to prompts and reassurance OR Withdrawn from most attempts to engage in care planning, support and/or daily activities	A person's mental state means they experience sustained periods of mood and anxiety problems which result in an inability to self-care which includes not eating or drinking Encouragement or reminders from others are not sufficient to manage the problems
High	Mood disturbance, hallucinations, anxiety or periods of distress which are having a severe impact on health and/or well-being OR Withdrawn from any attempts to engage in care planning, support and/or daily activities	A person has persistent psychotic symptoms which means they believe their care team and supporters are trying to control them which results in disengagement from all support and further decline in the person's mental health

Source: Adapted from DOH 2009d: 20.

Reminder Checklist: Psychological/Emotional

✓ Have you considered how the person's psychological health impacts upon their overall health and well-being?

✓ Have you explored how responsive the person's psychological needs are to intervention?

✓ Have you matched the person's assessed needs and presentation to the criteria set out in the CHC guidance to identify the level of need in this area against the framework?

DOMAIN: DRUG THERAPIES AND MEDICATION SYMPTOM CONTROL

The management of many psychological and mental health conditions may include a range of medications and prescribing regimes. It is well established that the management of medication, including possible side effects, is a very real issue (for example, see Adams and Scott 2001; Fakhoury et al. 2001; Smith et al. 2002; Barnes et al. 2007), with impacts such as weight gain and sexual dysfunction being well-documented problems with some psychiatric medications.

Medication administration and monitoring are often a key part of an individual's care and support plan, and regular reviews should be carried out as part of the overall support processes. In order to be eligible for CHC within this domain, the individual's experience of how their symptoms are managed and the intensity of those symptoms is an important consideration (where this affects other aspects of the individual's life, workers are directed to consider other domains particularly the psychological and emotional needs). In determining the level of need within this domain, the key indicator to be considered 'is the knowledge and skill required to manage the clinical need and the interaction of the medication in relation to the need' (DOH 2009d:71) that practitioners will need to consider.

Table 3.4 sets out the DOH guidance in relation to the nature, intensity, complexity and predictability of an individual's presentation and needs within this domain and provides some practical examples of what might be included in each level. This is not intended as an exhaustive list, but rather to provide a basis for social workers to start thinking about whether CHC may be an appropriate avenue to explore.

Table 3.4 Department of Health guidance in relation to the nature, intensity, complexity and predictability of an individual's presentation and needs (domain: drug therapies and medication symptom control)

Level	Description	Example
No need	Symptoms are managed effectively and without any problems and medication is not resulting in any unmanageable side effects	
Low	Requires supervision/ administration of and/or prompting with medication or has a physical, mental or cognitive impairment that requires support OR Mild pain that is predictable or associated with certain activities of daily living Pain and other symptoms do not impact on provision of care	A person regularly forgets to take their medication to manage their health condition This can be managed by the use of equipment, personal prompt or telehealth to provide a reminder service to make sure the person takes their medication as per the prescribing regime
Moderate	Requires administration of medication due to non-concordance or	A person's mental health state means that they are regularly non-concordant

(Continued overleaf)

Table 3.4 *Continued*

Level	Description	Example
	non-compliance, type of medication or route of medication Moderate pain which follows a predictable pattern, or other symptoms which are having a moderate effect on other domains or on the provision of care	with both mental health and physical medication and this occurs in a cycle with the fluctuations in their mental health condition Medication needs to be administered to maintain the person's health and well-being
High	Requires administration and monitoring of medication regime by a registered nurse, carer or care worker specifically trained for the task because there are risks associated with potential fluctuation of medical condition or mental state or the potential nature or severity of side-effects With monitoring the condition is usually not problematic to manage OR Moderate pain or other symptoms have a significant effect on other domains or the provision of care	A person requires daily administration of a controlled medication that requires specific training The person has a pattern of non-concordance as a result of side effects that can be adequately managed with support from trained carers/ nursing support which includes regular monitoring of effects and health and regular review of dosage levels in conjunction with the prescribing doctor
Severe	Requires administration and monitoring of medication regime by a registered	A person is non-concordant with medication as a result of severe side effects from a

nurse, carer or care worker specifically trained for the task because there are risks associated with potential fluctuation of medical condition or mental state or risks regarding the effectiveness of the medication, the potential nature or severity of side effects
The condition is usually problematic to manage even with monitoring
OR
Severe recurrent or constant pain which is not responding to treatment
OR
Risk of non-concordance with medication, placing the person at risk of relapse

range of prescribed medication
Side effects are difficult to manage and the person's mental health rapidly fluctuates as a result
Health monitoring is needed to continually assess both side effects and mental state and to maximise rapid responses when required
Specially trained support is needed to administer and monitor the person's response and concordance

Priority

A drug regime that requires daily monitoring by a registered nurse to ensure effective symptom and pain management associated with a rapidly changing or deteriorating condition
Unremitting and overwhelming pain despite all efforts to control pain effectively

A drug regime that requires daily monitoring by a registered nurse to ensure effective symptom and pain management associated with a rapidly changing or deteriorating condition
Unremitting and overwhelming pain despite all efforts to control pain effectively

Source: Adapted from DOH 2009d: 34.

Compliance and concordance are common issues within mental health services, and specific interventions are sometimes helpful to increase an individual's motivation and engagement with prescribing regimes. However, you should remember that there are many reasons why an individual does not take their medication as prescribed, and from a person-centred perspective it is important to ensure that these are explored and discussed with the individual, including considering other options where particular medications cause side-effects that impact upon the person's health, well-being and overall quality of life.

Non-concordance should not be viewed as the individual's problem which services need to address, or as a barrier to engagement – medication is one of many possible interventions, and the individual's views, aspirations and wishes should be taken into account in any assessment process, including those associated with drug therapies.

Reminder Checklist: Drug Therapies and Medication Symptom Control

✓ Have you considered how the person's medication and non-concordance with medication impact upon their overall health and well-being?

✓ Have you reviewed the side-effects experienced by the person and the impact of these on the person's general health and well-being?

✓ Have you assessed the level of intervention required to maintain concordance where appropriate?

✓ Have you considered issues of capacity and consent in relation to the person's concordance with medication?

✓ Have you matched the person's assessed needs and presentation to the criteria set out in the CHC guidance to identify the level of need in this area against the framework?

SUMMARY

As was the case with FACS in Chapter 2, although CHC is a national framework, local policies, procedures and templates will be in place that will need to be applied. CHC and FACS may at times overlap, and having an awareness of the criteria for each and how they are relevant can be helpful when considering how an individual's needs can best be met. The policy requirement for health and social care systems to work together is written across most policy guidance and best practice requirements, and thus social workers will need to understand and place in context the person's needs and support when undertaking any assessment for eligibility.

Identifying a primary health need can be a complex task, and your local health organisations may provide some assistance and clarity in terms of their expectations, and these should be followed wherever available. It is important to provide clear evidence to support your assessment, and to consider the whole range of support options, including their impact on the person's overall health. This chapter has provided some good practice suggestions to help shape your thinking and to support you in considering how CHC is applied to psychosocial needs. However, the full range of domains may need to be considered and readers are advised to review the CHC guidance published by the Department of Health for further information and guidance on working within the CHC criteria (DOH 2009a; 2009b; 2009c; 2009d).

Reminder Checklist: Applying NHS CHC

✓ Have you reviewed the individual's situation and identified whether there is a primary health need?
✓ Have you considered the person's needs in terms of nature, complexity, intensity and unpredictability and clearly

identified the impact of these needs on health and well-being?

✓ Have you familiarised yourself with your local thresholds and processes for CHC?

✓ Have you considered whether the person is eligible for CHC by completing the screening checklist (available from the DOH website)?

✓ Have you analysed the findings of your assessment, ensuring that you demonstrate how needs impact upon the individual's health?

✓ Have you considered capacity, consent and best interests in your assessment/screening and ensured that the principles of the MCA 2005 are applied?

✓ Have you considered all of the CHC domains and the individual's whole personal circumstances in relation to their health needs?

✓ Have you undertaken an analysis to identify where needs impact upon each other?

✓ Have you reflected the individual's wishes and aspirations throughout the assessment?

4 Common pitfalls and good practice suggestions

The advent of the personalisation agenda means that social workers have the opportunity to apply eligibility in more creative ways. Individual needs are the central element of assessment and funding applications, and, when working with psychosocial needs, social workers will need to be clear about how the individual's needs present a risk to their independence, in order to access social care funding support, while being aware of the possible continuing care needs and identifying when CHC may be an appropriate referral to make.

This chapter aims to provide an overview of common pitfalls and a range of good practice examples to assist social workers in considering the psychosocial needs of service users they are assessing for FACS eligibility. Personalisation focuses on recovery, social capital, choice and control, and thus requires workers to think in a more holistic way when considering eligibility and individual needs.

COMMON PITFALLS

One of the most common pitfalls experienced by practitioners is the inability to analyse and identify eligibility rather than risk of harm. In mental health, for example, risk factors are usually in relation to issues such as self-harm, self-neglect and risk of relapse, and while all of these may be relevant to eligibility, these need to be considered in relation to independence, not in relation to levels of harm. While one may contribute to the other, there is a marked difference between the two, and it is important that you are clear which framework is being assessed.

Example from Practice

This example was recorded in an assessment report being presented to a LA Community Care Funding Panel as the rationale for FACS eligibility.

Garth Johns is diagnosed with schizophrenia and has a history of self-harm and thoughts of suicide. He is assessed as being high risk in terms of harm to himself which occurs when Garth is low in mood. He needs regular monitoring of his mood and mental well-being to identify and manage his relapse indicators which include sleep disturbance and social withdrawal, both of which respond to talking therapy and medication.

While this statement may be clear and accurate about the individual's mental health needs, it would not be enough to justify funding eligibility. In order to form an argument for FACS eligibility, the assessment report needs to specifically address the FACS criteria and show how a personalised approach could be taken.

To overcome this common pitfall, you need to be clear about how the individual meets the risk to independence requirement. The statement above fails to do this as it is focused on the mental state of the individual, not their social care needs. Reframing the above example, you need to be specific and demonstrate, with evidence, how FACS applies in order to provide the best opportunity for the individual to qualify for the support they need.

The content of the assessment report for FACS should consider each area specifically and demonstrate how the appropriate criteria are met. In Garth's case, his eligibility against FACS would be as follows:

Garth Johns has an established diagnosis and an identified relapse pattern which presents a severe risk to his overall well-being. Garth is unable to maintain his self-care and his independence is at risk as a result of self-harm, self-neglect and social withdrawal.

■ *Family and Community Life – Critical*: Without monitoring and ongoing social support, Garth's mental health is likely to deteriorate, as demonstrated by his history of social withdrawal which includes occupation and being unable to maintain contact with his daughter without prompting and support.

- *Personal and Daily Routines – Substantial*: When low in mood, Garth is unable to maintain his self-care and regularly forgets to take his medication, this impacts upon his day-to-day routines, for example, personal care, sleeping and eating patterns, which increase Garth's risk of relapse in his mental state and his ability to live independently.
- *Health and Safety – Substantial*: Garth has a history of self-harm and thoughts of suicide when experiencing low mood, and experiences auditory hallucinations telling him to harm himself. As a result, Garth's health and safety are at times significantly compromised, with the risk of abuse and neglect being a significant concern.

Commentary

In most service contexts, risk assessment and management will be one of the central elements, and this can create confusion for workers who may have to navigate several sets of criteria. It is important to link the various processes; however, the focus needs to be upon the individual's independence and how their needs and strengths impact upon this. Individual well-being and prevention are both elements that are important considerations in a personalised approach, and it is the worker's role to undertake an analysis of the person's needs to identify and promote choice and control within the support planning and packages in line with the FACS eligibility criteria.

Good Practice Point: Independence

Remember that FACS eligibility is based upon the risk to a person's independence, and while other risk processes may operate in your service, in order to access social care funding support, the person's independence should be your focus.

On a more general level, the lack of analysis in the assessment process is another common pitfall that workers experience within the assessment and eligibility process. Assessments are not a list of things known about a person, they should instead be an analysis of how needs, strengths, resources and wishes interact, and what support is needed to assist the individual in achieving their goals and aspirations. In this process the Local Authority also should be assured that the individual's needs are eligible and this requires more than just information collection.

Example from Practice

Rebecca has been a mental health services user for a number of years, as she is diagnosed with bipolar disorder which is characterised by extreme highs and lows in mood which affect her thoughts and behaviour. Rebecca has been admitted to hospital several times when she is hypomanic (highs) as she becomes disinhibited and is unable to keep herself safe from danger within the community, both in terms of reckless behaviour and in her interactions with others. She has previously found admission to hospital very traumatic and would benefit from contingency planning to maximise her choice and control over her own situation and to ensure that she is able to sustain and build upon her current levels of independence.

Rebecca is assessed as eligible for FACS as her behaviour when manic means that her needs within the domain of health and safety are substantial. Within a personalised approach a plan was developed with Rebecca that identified her relapse patterns and what she would prefer to happen and if/when she became unwell or the risks to herself were too high to contain at home.

Plan

Rebecca and her social worker agree that alternatives to admission would be hugely beneficial if the risks to her health and safety could be more appropriately anticipated and managed.

Commentary

Demonstrating interrelation and interaction of needs and aspirations is a vital part of the assessment process. It is important that you consider how the assessed needs affect the person's situation and well-being, and what the consequences for their level of personal independence are if support is not provided.

> **Good Practice Point: Matching Needs and Policies**
>
> Make sure you set out the service user's needs in a way which matches your LA's policies and procedures, ensuring that you consider the criteria as an integral part of your assessment.

Social capital and universal services are both elements of a personalised approach. Workers will need to ask themselves and their service users whether a need is better met in an informal and/or mainstream setting, or is social care funding and/or CHC required to purchase services specifically to meet the assessed eligible need?

It is likely that an FACS funding panel will ask you, as the social worker or care manager, what has been considered, and without a rationale for why some options are not appropriate, it is likely that your funding application will be rejected unless you can prove that you have considered all the available and appropriate options. Therefore, it is much more effective to demonstrate your decision-making and wider considerations in the initial application and eligibility assessment rather than delaying the process by missing out a vital element of the process.

Good Practice Point: Domains and Levels

It is helpful to clearly state in your assessment which domains and at which level you have identified and assessed the needs.

As with many areas of life, it is helpful to be clear about what it is you are trying to evidence and demonstrate. Remember that personalised social care centres on individual needs, yet the FACS criteria are essentially an allocation system. It is up to you to represent the individual's situation in a way which the LA considers the individual to be eligible and hence supportable. You will need to ensure that you are familiar with your authority's thresholds and criteria as well as the overall FACS guidance and use these thresholds in your assessment and application practice to ensure you are able to articulate the individual's needs in a way which matches your local area requirements.

Reminder Checklist: Avoiding Common Pitfalls

✓ Have you considered risk to independence as well as risks to the person (or others) in your assessment and panel report/request?

✓ Have you clearly identified the domains in which the person's needs meet the substantial or critical levels?

✓ Have you familiarised yourself with local policies and thresholds and mapped the individual's needs against these as part of your assessment and decision-making process?

✓ Have you considered and documented the options, including informal and social support options, as well as purchasing services?

✓ Have you reflected the individual's (and their carer's/family's, if appropriate) wishes, goals and aspirations in your assessment and associated reports/requests?

✓ Have you provided an analysis of the person's needs, strengths and resources and considered the impact of these on their overall health and well-being?

While the delivery of social care aspires to be needs-led, this is very rarely the case in the context of dwindling budgets and resource allocation systems, and as therefore it is the responsibility of practitioners to maximise the opportunity to access support for their service users and to consider creative ways in which to address prevention and social support needs within their authority's requirements.

INFORMATION AS A PERSONALISED SERVICE

Assessment forms, thresholds and practice guidance should all be available locally, along with information about how to access FACS funding. In a personalised approach, information and involvement are both a significant focus, and in order to maximise individual choice and control, it is important that you are able to support informed decision-making and collaborative support planning with individuals, both of which require you as the worker to be familiar with and able to guide individuals through the assessment and eligibility pathways.

Good Practice Point: Resource Allocation System

Familiarise yourself with your authority's resource allocation system (RAS) so you are able to explain it to service users and carers where appropriate.

Example from Practice

Mr and Mrs Jones are both 73 are have never accessed state support before. They are anxious about what is available and are keen to remain at home together for as long as possible. Mr Jones was diagnosed with dementia several years ago and has been accessing therapeutic support and memory clinics via his local health trust.

Mr Jones' memory and orientation have been deteriorating over the past few months and Mrs Jones is finding it increasingly difficult to care for him. She has been referred to social services for a carer assessment and Mr Jones' needs are to be reassessed under FACS to ascertain whether he is eligible for social care support. They are very anxious about the whole process and are requesting information on the range of options available, on what personal budgets are and how they can manage them, and what they may be eligible for in terms of support options, benefits and other income sources. They are very worried about the means-testing element of assessment.

Plan

Mr and Mrs Jones are provided with a range of written information in relation to assessment, carer support and FACS. The social worker spends some time going over this information and answering their questions. Advocacy and carer support information is also provided and Mrs Jones is taken through the brokerage and RAS processes to explain what happens, when and why.

Outcome

An assessment under FACS is undertaken with Mr Jones and a carer's assessment is carried out with Mrs Jones. Once completed, the worker returns to see Mr and Mrs Jones with the assessment documentation and the next stage of the process is explained to them.

Commentary

In the case of Mr and Mrs Jones, there was a significant level of anxiety about what an assessment and receiving services (if eligible) from social care could involve, and in this instance detailed information formed a service in itself as it enabled the Jones to have choice and control over their situation. Eligibility for FACS is just one element of the process, and workers need to ensure that they are considering needs in a wider context. The NHS and Community Care Act 1990 places the assessment function in the context of a service, and thus, in order to achieve a personalised approach the person needs to be fully involved and informed so they are able to participate as appropriate in each situation.

Good Practice Point: Incorporate the Person's Views

In order to maximise involvement, the person and their supporters need to be informed and their views incorporated into the assessment process.

Reminder Checklist: Providing Information

✓ Have you explained the process and eligibility requirements to the person?

✓ Have you provided written and verbal information in a form which is appropriate for the person/their carer and family?

✓ Have you considered capacity and consent in the context of providing information and undertaking your assessment?

✓ How are you ensuring the person is involved and their views and aspirations are reflected in your practice?

SUMMARY

While practice examples have been provided throughout this book, this chapter has considered some additional issues and how to avoid some of the common pitfalls in assessment for eligibility.

Personalisation support involves creative approaches to meeting individual needs, and in order to apply this to the FACS framework you will need to be clear about how needs interact and impact upon the person and their situation. This is particularly the case with psycho-social needs as these are usually far more complex and interrelated.

As the assessor, the onus is placed upon you to demonstrate and evidence the impact of the individual's needs on their personal independence, and at times of stretched budgets it is vital that you are able to accurately and appropriately apply criteria in order to secure support for individual service users and carers.

Reminder Checklist: Common Pitfalls and Good Practice

✓ Have you reviewed your assessment to make sure you have met all the local requirements?

✓ Have you provided all the relevant information to relevant parties?

✓ Have you been explicit with individuals and outlined the processes?

✓ Have you fully documented and analysed assessed needs?

✓ Have you clearly set out your recommendations?

✓ Have you considered and demonstrated capacity, consent and involvement?

✓ Have you ensured needs are explicitly linked to eligibility criteria?

✓ Have you provided appropriate supporting information to justify your assessment?

✓ Have you considered appropriate support plans to meet assessed needs?

✓ Have you fully involved the person and their supporters in any risk assessment and management plans?

5 Further reading and resources

A comprehensive range of references are provided in this book, and readers are advised to review and familiarise themselves both with their local policies and procedures and the national frameworks in order to support their practice.

The Department of Health publishes a range of guidance and tools in relation to both FACS and CHC and these can be accessed via the DOH website: www.dh.gov.uk.

Good Practice Point: DOH Website

Access the DOH website and review the guidance and tools available to support screening and assessment for FACS and CHC eligibility prior to starting your assessment.

In addition to official eligibility information, a range of good practice guides, evidence-based studies and research and practice development tools relevant to applying eligibility within a personalised context are available in both hard copy and electronically, and this final section provides information in relation to some subject-specific resources which may be helpful for social workers in practice.

FAIR ACCESS TO CARE SERVICES (FACS) RESOURCES

A range of information both online and via books/articles is available to support your understanding and application of the FACS criteria and to guide your thinking in relation to applying FACS to your assessments and practice. Some resources which are particularly helpful are detailed below. Readers are advised to access and familiarise themselves with their organisational information and guidance as a priority.

■ The Social Care Institute for Excellence (SCIE) has developed a range of e-learning resources to support practitioners working across social care. These resources include a module on FACS which is free to access and which covers the 2010 FACS framework and how these can be applied to personalised outcomes. The resource is available online at: http://www.scie.org.uk/publications/elearning/fairaccesstocareservices/index.asp.

■ SCIE also publishes a range of information, including a leaflet, which details the FACS system and considers the implications of the Dilnott Commission Review. These resources are available online at: http://www.scie.org.uk/topic/keyissues/accesstoservices.

Other resources and information that may be helpful in supporting a personalised approach to FACS include:

■ CQC (2011) *The State of Care Report 2010/11*. London: CQC. Available at: http://www.cqc.org.uk/public/reports-surveys-and-reviews/reports/state-care-report-2010/11.

■ Lymbery, M. (2010) A new vision for adult social care? Continuities and change in the care of older people. *Critical Social Policy*, 30(1): 5–26.

NHS CONTINUING HEALTHCARE RESOURCES

Department of Health publications provide the most up-to-date information and guidance available on NHS Continuing Healthcare and these are referenced throughout Chapter 3 in order to signpost you to the relevant information. In addition to these, resources that may be helpful in practice include:

■ NHS Choices publish a range of information about CHC and this can be accessed online at: http://www.nhs.uk/CarersDirect/guide/practicalsupport/Pages/NHSContinuingCare.aspx.
■ The Alzheimer's Society details information that may apply to dementia. Their information and resources can be accessed online at: http://www.alzheimers.org.uk/site/scripts/documents_info.php?documentID=399.

PERSONALISATION RESOURCES

There are many resources available regarding personalisation approaches and agendas, and books, research articles and websites can provide a wide range of information to support your practice. Some of these which are particularly helpful are included here, and readers are advised to access their organisation's websites and intranets to familiarise themselves with their locally published resources.

■ In-Control is a project which was established at the outset of personalisation, and a range of trials, tools and good practice guidance was developed as a result in partnership with service users and local authorities. The In-Control website provides access to a full suite of information to support practice and can be accessed online at: http://www.in-control.org.uk/.
■ SCIE have developed a full suite of resources and information in relation to personalisation which can be accessed online at: http://www.scie.org.uk/topic/keyissues/personalisation. Resources include information, research reports and a range of tools for use across the full range of service user groups.
■ Safeguarding has been a significant concern within the personalisation agenda, and the Department of Health has

published guidance to provide practical support in this area. The guide is available online at: http://www.dh.gov.uk/prod_consum_ dh/groups/dh_digitalassets/@dh/@en/@ps/documents/digitalasset/ dh_121671.pdf.

■ The Think Local, Act Personal Partnership is a consortium of 30 organisations representing various stakeholders in the development of personalisation and community support. The partnership's website includes a range of information to support personalisation including topic guides, tools and resources, networking opportunities and details of events. The site can be accessed online at: http://www.thinklocalactpersonal.org.uk.

■ *Community Care* magazine has published a review undertaken jointly with Unison, detailing the progress and state of personalisation across social care in the UK. The report and a range of other information about personalisation can be found online at: http://www.communitycare.co.uk/static-pages/articles/ The-state-of-personalisation-in-adult-social-care/.

■ The National Mental Health Development Unit (NMHDU) ceased to exist in 2011. However, prior to its closure it commissioned and published a helpful resource considering personalisation in mental health and how a systems approach could be taken and the document is still available online at: http:// www.nmhdu.org.uk/nmhdu/en/our-work/personalisation-in- mental-health-emerging-programme/paths-to-personalisation/.

Other resources such as books and articles that you may find helpful are:

Bogg, D. (2010) *Mental Health and Personalisation: Themes and Issues in Recovery-Based Mental Health Care and Support*. Brighton: Pavilion.

Glasby, J. and Littlechild, R. (2009) *Direct Payments and Personal Budgets: Putting Personalisation into Practice*. Bristol: The Policy Press.

Glendinning, C., Moran, N., Challis, D. et al. (2011) Personalisation and part- nership: competing objectives in English adult social care? The Individual Budget Pilot Projects and the NHS. *Social Policy & Society*, 10(2): 151–62.

Newman, S. (2009) *Personalisation: Practical Thoughts and Ideas from People Making It Happen*. Brighton: Pavilion.

Sanderson, H. and Lewis, J. (2010) *A Practical Guide to Delivering Personalisation: Person-Centred Practice in Health and Social Care*. London: Jessica Kingsley.

Scown, S. and Sanderson, H. (2011) *Making It Personal for Everyone: From Block Contracts to Individual Service Contracts*. Stockport: Dimensions.

Reminder Checklist: Further Reading and Resources

✓ Have you familiarised yourself with your local policies and procedures?

✓ Have you reviewed and familiarised yourself with national guidance and available tools?

✓ Have you reviewed and identified the gaps in your knowledge and identified actions and resources you would benefit from accessing in relation to your assessments of eligible needs?

✓ Have you considered how you can apply personalisation to FACS in your practice context?

References

Adams, J. and Scott, J. (2001) Predicting medication adherence in severe mental disorders, *Acta Psychiatrica Scandinavica*, 101(2): 119–24.

Barnes, T.R.E., Paton, C., Cavanagh, M-R., Hancock, E. and Taylor, D.M. (2007) A UK audit of screening for the metabolic side effects of antipsychotics in community patients, *Schizophrenia Bulletin*, 33(6): 1397–403.

City of York Council (2011) *Eligibility Criteria* [online]. Available at: http://www.york.gov.uk/health/Disabilities/Needs_assessment/Eligibility_criteria/.

Clements, L. and Thompson, P. (2011) *Community Care and the Law*, 5th edn. London: Legal Action Group.

Croydon Social Services (undated) *Fair Access to Care Services* [online]. Available at: http://www.croydon.gov.uk/contents/departments/healthsocial/pdf/fairaccess.pdf.

Dilnott Commission (2011a) *Fairer Care Funding: The Report of the Commission on Funding of Care and Support.* London: TSO. Available at: https://www.wp.dh.gov.uk/carecommission/files/2011/07/Fairer-Care-Funding-Report.pdf.

Dilnott Commission (2011b) *Fairer Care Funding: Policy Briefing Note.* Available at: http://www.dilnotcommission.dh.gov.uk/files/2011/09/Technical-Briefing-Note.pdf.

DOH (2001) *Carers and Disabled Children Act 2000: Carers and People with Parental Responsibility for Disabled Children: Practice Guidance.* London: DOH. Available at: http://www.dh.gov.uk/prod_consum_dh/groups/dh_digitalassets/documents/digitalasset/dh_085030.pdf.

DOH (2002) *Fair Access to Care Services: Guidance on Eligibility Criteria for Adult Social Care.* LAC (2002) 13. London: DOH. Available at: http://www.dh.gov.uk/en/Publicationsandstatistics/Publications/PublicationsPolicyAndGuidance/DOH_4009653.

DOH (2003) *Fair Access to Care Services: Practice Guidance.* London: DOH. Available at: http://www.dh.gov.uk/prod_consum_dh/groups/dh_digitalassets/@dh/@en/documents/digitalasset/dh_4019734.pdf.

DOH (2005) *Independence, Well-Being and Choice: Our Vision for the Future of Social Care for Adults in England.* London: DOH. Available at: http://

www.dh.gov.uk/prod_consum_dh/groups/dh_digitalassets/@dh/@en/documents/digitalasset/dh_4106478.pdf.

DOH (2006) *Our Health, Our Care, Our Say: A New Direction for Community Services*. London: TSO.

DOH (2007) *Best Practice in Managing Risk: Principles and Evidence for Best Practice in the Assessment and Management of Risk to Self and Others in Mental Health Services*. London: TSO.

DOH (2008) *Transforming Social Care*, LAC (DOH) (2008) 1. London: DOH. Available at: http://www.dh.gov.uk/prod_consum_dh/groups/dh_digitalassets/documents/digitalasset/dh_082139.pdf.

DOH (2009a) *The National Framework for NHS Continuing Healthcare and NHS-Funded Nursing Care: July 2009* (revised). London: DOH. Available at: http://www.dh.gov.uk/prod_consum_dh/groups/dh_digitalassets/documents/digitalasset/dh_103161.pdf.

DOH (2009b) *NHS Continuing Healthcare Checklist*. London: DOH. Available at: http://www.dh.gov.uk/prod_consum_dh/groups/dh_digitalassets/documents/digitalasset/dh_103328.pdf.

DOH (2009c) *NHS Continuing Healthcare (Responsibilities) Directions 2009: NHS Act 2006*, LA SS Act 1970. London: DOH. Available at: http://www.dh.gov.uk/en/Publicationsandstatistics/Publications/PublicationsLegislation/DOH_106176.

DOH (2009d) *Decision Support Tool for NHS Continuing Healthcare*. London: TSO. Available at: http://www.dh.gov.uk/prod_consum_dh/groups/dh_digitalassets/documents/digitalasset/dh_103329.pdf.

DOH (2010a) *Prioritising Need in the Context of Putting People First: A Whole System Approach to Eligibility for Social Care: Guidance on Eligibility Criteria for Adult Social Care, England 2010*. London: DOH. Available at: http://www.dh.gov.uk/en/Publicationsandstatistics/Publications/PublicationsPolicyAndGuidance/DOH_113154.

DOH (2010b) *NHS Continuing Healthcare Practice Guidance*. London: DOH. Available at: http://www.dh.gov.uk/en/Publicationsandstatistics/Publications/PublicationsPolicyAndGuidance/DOH_115133.

DOH (2010c) *A Vision for Adult Social Care: Capable Communities and Active Citizens*. London: DOH. Available at: http://www.dh.gov.uk/en/Publicationsandstatistics/Publications/PublicationsPolicyAndGuidance/DOH_121508.

Fakhoury, W.K.H., Wright, D. and Wallace, M. (2001) Prevalence and extent of distress of adverse effects of antipsychotics among callers to a United Kingdom National Mental Health Helpline, *International Clinical Psychopharmacology*, 16(3): 153–62.

Hertfordshire County Council (2003) *Fair Access to Care Services in Hertfordshire: Adult Social Care Eligibility Criteria Guidance Notes for Staff*. Available at: http://www.hertsdirect.org/statweb/compaperarchive/archive/older_meetings/Reports/103/483/2.pdf.

HM Government (2007) *Putting People First: A Shared Vision and Commitment to the Transformation of Adult Social Care*. London: TSO. Available at: http://www.dh.gov.uk/prod_consum_dh/groups/dh_digital-assets/@dh/@en/documents/digitalasset/dh_081119.pdf.

HM Government (2011) *No Health Without Mental Health: A Cross-Governmental Mental Health Outcome Strategy for People of All Ages*. London:TSO.Availableat:http://www.dh.gov.uk/en/Publicationsandstatistics/Publications/PublicationsPolicyAndGuidance/DOH_123766.

Langan, J. and Lidlow, V. (2004) *Living with Risk: Mental Health Service User Involvement in Risk Assessment and Management*. Bristol: Policy Press.

Mandelstam, M. (2009) *Community Care Practice and the Law*, 4th edn. London: Jessica Kingsley Publishers.

NHS (2009) *NHS Continuing Healthcare and NHS-Funded Nursing Care: Public Information Booklet*. London: TSO. Available at: http://www.dh.gov.uk/prod_consum_dh/groups/dh_digitalassets/documents/digitalasset/dh_106229.pdf.

NHS Information Centre (2011) *Personal Social Services Expenditure Report 2009–10*. Available at: http://www.ic.nhs.uk/webfiles/publications/009_Social_Care/pss0910expfinal/pss0910updateOct2011/Personal_Social_Services_Expenditure_Report_2009_10.pdf.

Smith, S., O'Keane, V. and Murray, R. (2002) Sexual dysfunction in patients taking conventional antipsychotic medication. *British Journal of Psychiatry*, 181: 49–55.

CASES CITED

R v Bexley NHS Care Trust, ex parte Grogan [2006] EWHC 44 (Admin), available at: http://www.bailii.org/ew/cases/EWHC/Admin/2006/44.html.

R v Gloucestershire County Council, ex parte Barry [1997] 2 All ER 1, House of Lords.

R v North Devon Health Authority, ex parte Pamela Coughlan [1999] EWCA Civ 1871, available at: http://www.bailii.org/ew/cases/EWCA/Civ/1999/1871.html.

Index